CHURCH PLANTING

By the same Author

Alfred Dye, Minister of the Gospel
Robert Mackintosh: Theologian of Integrity
God Our Father
The Great Debate: Calvinism, Arminianism and Salvation
Church Planting: A Study of Westmorland Nonconformity
Theology in Turmoil

CHURCH PLANTING

A Study of Westmorland Nonconformity

ALAN P. F. SELL

WIPF & STOCK · Eugene, Oregon

Wipf and Stock Publishers
199 W 8th Ave, Suite 3
Eugene, OR 97401

Church Planting
A Study of Westmoreland Nonconformity
By Sell, Alan P.F.

ISBN 13: 978-1-57910-127-5
Publication date 6/23/1998
Previously published by H. E. Walter Limited,, 1986

To
Bridget, Judith and Jonathan –
all Kendal born

CONTENTS

ABBREVIATIONS

BHST	*Baptist Historical Society Transactions*, 1908/9–1920/1; continued as *Baptist Quarterly*.
BQ	W. C. Braithwaite, *The Beginnings of Quakerism*, 2nd edn., revised by Henry J. Cadbury, Cambridge, 1970.
Besse's Sufferings	Joseph Besse, *A Collection of the Sufferings of the people called Quakers*, 2 vols., 1753.
CR	A. G. Matthews, *Calamy Revised*, Oxford, 1934.
CHST	*Congregational Historical Society Transactions*, 1901–72.
CYB	*Congregational Year Book*, 1846–1972.
DNB	*Dictionary of National Biography*.
ECW	B. Nightingale, *The Ejected of 1662 in Cumberland and Westmorland*, 2 vols., Manchester, 1911.
EM	*The Evangelical Magazine*, 1793–1904.
EQL	G. F. Nuttall, *Early Quaker Letters from the Swarthmore Mss to 1660*, unpublished typescript, 1952.
EQW	Hugh Barbour and Arthur Roberts, *Early Quaker Writings*, Grand Rapids, 1973.
FPT	Norman Penney, ed., *The First Publishers of Truth*, 1907.
JFHS	*Journal of the Friends' Historical Society*, 1903/4–
KK	J. F. Curwen, *Kirkbie-Kendal*, Kendal, 1900.
LN	B. Nightingale, *Lancashire Nonconformity*, I, Manchester and London, n.d. but preface has 1890.
LPQ	Rufus M. Jones, *The Later Periods of Quakerism*, 2 vols., 1921.
LR	John F. Curwen, *The Later Records relating to North Westmorland or the Barony of Appleby*, Cumberland and Westmorland Antiquarian and Archaeological Society Record Series, VIII, Kendal, 1932.
Nicholson ms.	Ms. of an unfinished book by J. Walker Nicholson on nonconformity in the east of Westmorland. Owned by Mrs. M. R. Dent, Sedbergh.
N & B	Joseph Nicolson and Richard Burn, *The History and Antiquities of the Counties of Cumberland and Westmorland*, 1777.
ONK	Francis Nicholson and Ernest Axon, *The Older Nonconformity in Kendal*, Kendal, 1915.

PWHS	*Proceedings of the Wesley Historical Society*, 1897/8–
SPQ	W. C. Braithwaite, *The Second Period of Quakerism*, 2nd edn., prepared by H. J. Cadbury, Cambridge, 1961.
VCH	*Victoria County History*.

PREFACE

Church planting is a topic high on the agenda of many Christians throughout the world, and not least in Britain. More than ever before the realisation that the whole world is a mission field presses home, and the question of the fostering of a Christian presence in unchurched areas cannot but arise. In such a climate a case study of the origins and growth of Christian groups in a given area ought to be of more than purely antiquarian interest. I shall show that in the past churches have been formed in a number of ways: political circumstances led to ejection; conscience prompted secession; or a deliberate attempt was made by Christians to go forward in mission. The careful study of the fathers' successes and failures may be instructive to the sons.

My general interest in nonconformity is long-standing; my engagement with Westmorland is a direct result of the proximity to the county of my first pastorate, Sedbergh and Dent. In this book I seek to recount the origins, and to trace the development of those nonconformist groups which are, or have been, represented in Westmorland.

A writer on a subject of this kind is dependent to a considerable degree upon the willing co-operation of others. I should like to thank the following for having answered queries and, or, for having made materials available: Mr. D. C. L. Holland of the Library of the House of Commons; Mr. John Creasey of Dr. Williams's Library, London; Dr. F. Taylor and Mr. D. W. Riley of the John Rylands University Library, Manchester; Miss S. J. Macpherson, Archivist in Charge, County Record Office, Kendal; Messrs. J. Foster, C. Wood and A. R. Worsley of the Public Library, Kendal; Mr. H. W. Hodgson of Carlisle Public Library, the staff of the Central Library; Birmingham; Miss J. M. Owen of Sion College, the late Mr. B. Honess of the Congregational Library, London; The

Revd. G. W. Rusling and Miss Neville of the Baptist Union of Great Britain and Ireland; The Revd. Dr. J. C. Bowmer and Miss D. Baslington of the Methodist Archives and Research Centre, London; Mr. Jon North of the Library of the Society of Friends, London; Esther Williams and Joan Walford of the Library, Woodbrooke, Birmingham; Miss F. Williams, Librarian, Selly Oak Colleges, Birmingham; Mrs. L. Smith of the Library of West Midlands College of Higher Education, Walsall; Miss W. M. Burra, Secretary of the Westmorland Group of Baptist Churches; Mrs. M. R. Dent of Sedbergh, who kindly loaned the *Nicholson ms.*; The Revds. Sydney Cook, J. G. Hobbs, W. E. Moore and B. R. White (Baptists); Mr. E. Parker, Secretary of the Northern Baptist Association; Mr. J. Robinson of Egglesburn; The Revds. R. Buick Knox, Andrew Hodgson, the late J. E. Newport, G. F. Nuttall, the late G. P. Smailes, D. G. Stewart and G. M. Taylor (United Reformed Church); The Revd. G. R. Buckley (Unitarian); Mr. G. D. Braithwaite and Miss E. A. Winrow, Archivist and Membership Secretary respectively of the Carlisle Methodist district; Mr. E. A. Rose; Mr. Kirkby of the Methodist Department for Chapel Affairs; The Revds. W. Blackburn, G. W. Dolbey (Department for Chapel Affairs), M. Wesley Earl (Chairman, Carlisle Methodist district), Jeffrey W. Harris, J. Harrod, H. Stanley Hills, K. Mackenzie, J. A. E. Martin, John P. Monkhouse, Frank Robbins, Brian White and Raymond Wood (Methodists); Messrs. J. W. Marshall and A. W. Murdoch (Brethren); Pastor J. P. Metcalfe (Pentecostal); The Revd. J. T. George of the Congregational Union of Scotland; The Revd. Dr. J. M. Henry of the Congregational Union of Ireland; The Revd. H. Ethall of the Union of Welsh Independents; Pearl D. M. Lamb of the Religious Society of Friends in Ireland. I am also grateful to my former colleague Mr. Christopher Aylott of the Department of Mathematics, West Midlands College, for undertaking the calculations presented in chapter V; and to Professor W. R. Ward of the University of Durham for reading my work and encouraging me towards publication.

To three of the above special thanks are due: Miss W. M. Burra and the Revd. John P. Monkhouse read and commented helpfully upon the first draft of my Baptist and Methodist material respectively; and the Revd. Dr. G. F. Nuttall not only read both the earlier draft and the final revision of my work, but also directed me to sources of which I had not been aware, and kindly supplied relevant extracts from Whitefield's letters and from the Doddridge *mss.*

I am grateful to Miss I. Brunskill of Sedbergh for her confidence that this book *would* one day be published, and to my Publisher. I also wish to thank the trustees and officers of The Curwen Archives Trust, The Hibbert Trust, The Marc Fitch Fund, and The United Reformed Church History Society for the financial assistance which has helped to ensure its appearance. Finally, it seemed entirely appropriate that the one who produced those to whom the book is dedicated should produce the sketches which illustrate it. Accordingly, I thank my wife.

Alan P. F. Sell
Department of Theology
World Alliance of reformed Churches
Geneva

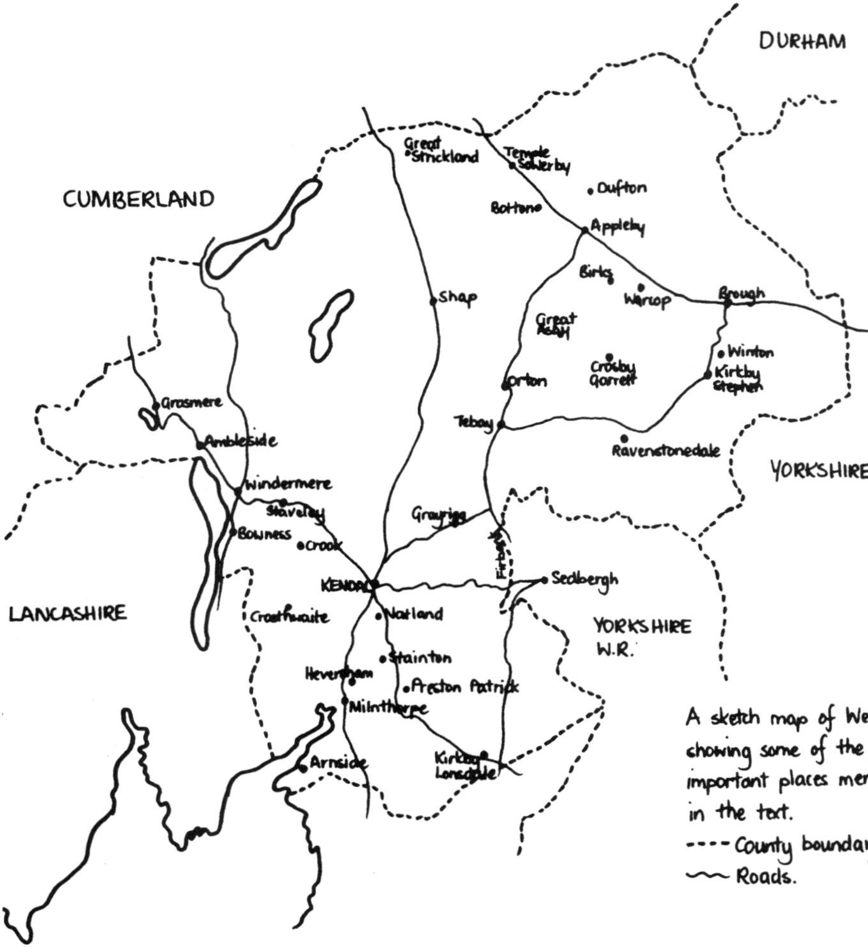

A sketch map of Westmorland, showing some of the more important places mentioned in the text.

---- County boundary.

~~ Roads.

I – INTRODUCTION

Church history comes in packages of widely differing sizes and shapes. There are accounts of individual local churches, often lovingly written by those whose place of worship they are. At the other extreme are volumes which treat of whole periods in the life of the Church at large. In between are books which treat of one denomination in its national, and sometimes in its international, relations. The present study is localised geographically, but not individualised denominationally. It is an attempt to trace the origins and expansion of nonconformity in one county, and to see what picture emerges when the several relevant communions are considered side by side. Our work is therefore narrower in scope than the complete denominational history; and wider than the latter in its attempt to consider each member of a family of denominations in roughly equal depth. We shall not be so specific as to describe a local chapel's architecture, communion plate, organ, and the like. Parallel denominational movements are what are here investigated. We shall seek to answer such questions as, when, and whence came nonconformity to Westmorland? How did the several denominations fare, and what is their present representation in, the county?

By 'Westmorland' in this book we mean the county of that name prior to the reorganisation of local government in 1974. Personal affection for the area aside, this county is selected because in one sense it is compassable, and in another sense it has not always been so. The county is compassable in terms of area, and the Friends, Old Dissent-Congregationalism, the Baptists and the Methodists are all represented there. But from the point of view of terrain, and of relative geographical isolation, Westmorland was by no means readily compassable in the past. As Richard S. Ferguson reminds us, 'Roads, in the year 1660, there were in

Cumberland and Westmorland but few, and those mostly traversed by packhorses alone. Public conveyances were none ... Sir Philip Musgrave writes to Sir Joseph Williamson that he has difficulty in getting up to Parliament because "the Northern Alps are covered with snow" '[1] In 1753 Westmorland's first Turnpike Act was in force, and by 1777, as Nicolson and Burn inform us, no fewer than seven turnpike roads passed through Kendal.[2] Whilst these helped to carry the evangelical revival to the Lakes and elsewhere in the county, the fact remains that non-indigenous nonconformity of whatever kind had to make a real effort to reach these remote parts. An examination of the different routes taken will add interest to our story.

Some aspects of nonconformity's story in Westmorland have been well covered: the Friends, the Congregationalists and the Unitarians have been ably served by Braithwaite, Nightingale, and Nicholson and Axon respectively. The Baptists and, to a lesser extent, the Methodists have not fared as well – certainly more collecting and collating has had to be done as far as they are concerned. Where possible the findings of others have been used, compared, and acknowledged. Our List of Sources has been set out in such a way as to show that approximately two thirds of the published items we have consulted appeared over fifty years ago. Many of these are now scarce – a fact which in itself more than justifies our re-telling of those parts of the tale that have already been told. Moreover, the overwhelming majority of our sources are limited by particular denominational and/or geographical interests. We have attempted to fill gaps in the total account, and to provide for the first time a synoptic view of the origins and development of nonconformity in Westmorland.

Now concerning the term 'nonconformity'. As already implied, we have in mind in this book Protestant, and not Roman Catholic, nonconformity; and we include the Methodists. Doubtless John Wesley was ever, emotionally and doctrinally, a loyal Anglican; he was as suspicious of hidebound and heterodox Dissent as many dissenters were of his 'enthusiasm'; he did not go to meeting. Politically, too, his Tory principles inclined him against largely Whig Dissent. Nevertheless many of his actions entailed dissent – not least his eventual advocacy of the licensing of chapels under the Toleration Act; and his ordaining of men first for Scotland, then for America and finally for England. And although, on the other hand, the Wesleyans did not, for example, send representatives to the inaugural meetings of the British and Foreign Bible Society in 1804, on the ground that they were already represented by the Anglican bishops, they were by that time *de facto* nonconformists, and their New Connexion brethren were overtly so. The subsequent divisions within the Methodist family further generally eroded Methodist-Anglican links, as did Methodist suspicion of the ritualism and Tractarianism which were soon to develop within the Mother Church. The campaigns for the removal of political, social and educational disabilities brought Methodists and Old Dissent ever closer together in a common cause; and by the end of the century it was the *Wesleyan*, Hugh Price Hughes, who was the universally acknowledged prophet of the *nonconformist* conscience. Much more could be said on the standing of Methodism *vis a vis* the Church of England and Dissent, but we feel that the presence of the Methodists in this book is adequately justified. Certainly it would have been much harder to have justified their exclusion!

Having thus admitted the Methodists, we find that they exemplify two problems which confront us, and present a third. The first problem, concerning nomenclature, arises from the fact that it is only with the passage of time that denominational titles become established sufficiently to obviate ambiguity and confusion. In the seventeenth century the terms 'Quaker' and 'Anabaptist' were used loosely, and often pejoratively, of nonconformists in general: 'Quakers and phanaticks' is a fairly common conjunction of epithets.[3] Again, the designation 'Independent' was employed indiscriminately of both paedobaptists and anabaptists, and even at times of the most radical sectaries. This breadth of usage was, no doubt, among the factors which prompted the Savoy Fathers to describe their Delcaration of 1658 as being one pertaining to 'the *Congregational* Churches in England'. It is the term 'Presbyterian', however, which has provoked the greatest amount of scholarly discussion. The question is whether 'Presbyterian' was anything *more* than a name in Westmorland after the Restoration and prior to the second half of the eighteenth century. Nightingale goes so far as to argue that 'as an organised religious force in the country [Presbyterianism] had ceased to exist long before 1660.'[4] In the highly important first chapter of *ECW* he makes out his case, against such writers as Drysdale and Macphail, that even during its established hey-day pre-Restoration Presbyterianism was never representative of the popular religion of the country; that Presbyterian polity was never, except in Lancashire, London and a few southern and eastern counties, seriously put into practice; and that since classes (a further loosely-used term) were few and far between, ordination services were frequently conducted by groups of ministers voluntarily summoned for the purpose, and comprising Presbyterians and Independents indiscriminately. The mooted Kendal classis of c.1645 never became operational, and such Associations as were established – as, for example, the Cumberland and Westmorland Association of 1656 – were voluntary, and barely continued after the Restoration, even if they survived at all. Nightingale provides further evidence to show that the Indulgence Licences of 1672, and extant accounts of post-Restoration ordination arrangements, bear witness to similar ambiguities. He does not claim that there were no points of difference as between post-Restoration Presbyterians and Independents, but simply that 'these divergencies were not sufficient to justify the use of the name [Presbyterian]; that the Presbyterian idea had so far emptied itself of its contents as to represent neither the Presbyterianism of Commonwealth days nor the Presbyterianism of modern history . . .'[5] Although many Presbyterians conformed at the Restoration, partly because they had no serious theological objections to establishment, and partly because of personal factors or patronal pressure, the name outlived the idea because, after all, the system *had* been the established vogue. Indeed, the name survived, by contraction, to indicate those of 'a spiritual serious way of worship'.[6]

In view of all this, the assertion of J. Hay Colligan to the effect that the 'early and marked characteristics' of the Westmorland dissenting congregations was Presbyterian, and that 'among several congregations Independency appears in the decandent stages of the congregational life' seems strangely unsubtle and unduly blunt.[7] It would be more accurate to say of the four oldest Westmorland dissenting causes that whereas they were originally nominally, though not politically, Presbyterian, a rather isolationist spirit overcame Ravenstonedale, Stainton and Crook as the eighteenth century progressed, whilst Kendal became Unitarian. That numerical weakness and geographical isolation contributed to the isolationist tendency is clear, but it is perverse to regard a distortion of Independency as if it were the genuine article; and this is what Colligan does by implication.

So, finally, to 'Methodist'. It is well known that this term was one of a number of epithets originally applied to the members of that Oxford Holy Club, established in 1728, to which John and Charles Wesley belonged. In England the term has come to be almost exclusively applied to the Arminian heirs of the Wesleys. We should not forget, however, that when Charles Wesley took the unprecendented step of inviting a servitor, George Whitefield, to the meetings of the Club, he facilitated the birth of that Calvinistic strain of Methodism which, through Whitefield and those who thought like him, has ever since been discernible, albeit *comparatively* weakly, in England. Nor should we overlook the fact that many who remained within the Anglican fold after John Wesley's death and into the nineteenth century, were influenced by the Evangelical Revival in the direction of Methodist attitudes and disciplines.

These last two propositions may be illustrated by reference to Kendal. In the first half of the nineteenth century a congregation of Calvinistic Methodists met over a period of twenty years in the Kirkland Conventicle. Their leader was Mr. George Robinson, a grocer. Again, c.1823, the theatre which was later to be occupied by the Revd. Robert Wilson and the Scotch Seceders, was closed. It was generally held that the demise of the theatre was directly attributable to the activities of the Revd. William Whitelock of St. George's Chapel, Market Place, who, among other things, published a tract entitled, *The Great Assize or the Day of Judgment,* in the format of a play bill. For such enthusiasm he was known to some – and not least to his co-religionists at the Parish Church – as 'that silly Methody man'.[8]

The second problem which the Methodists exemplify is that concerning the relative proportions of the materials at our disposal. Though comparatively late in the field, they have covered the county as no other nonconformist body has done. At one extreme we have dozens of Methodist chapels; at the other, the one Unitarian chapel in Kendal. The upshot is that our treatment of the latter will necessarily have more the appearance of a chapel history (albeit a selective one) than our treatment of the former. Our rule has been to concentrate upon individual chapels only to the extent that this enables us to illustrate the origins and growth of the denominations concerned, or in cases where there are especially significant ecclesiastical, theological or other reasons for so doing. Again, it is not surprising that there is much more material available concerning the largest town, Kendal, than concerning any other place in the county. This said, however, it should be remembered that neither Arminian nor Clavinistic Baptists, nor the precursors of the United Methodists ever became firmly established in the town. In Appleby alone did the three Methodist denominations: Wesleyan, Primitive and United, exist side by side.

The new problem which the Methodists pose concerns *their* connexional disregard of county boundaries, and *our* desire to confine our attention to Westmorland. We have had to bear in mind that Blencarn and Spital (Kirkby Stephen and Appleby circuit) are in Cumberland and Yorkshire respectively; that Cowan Bridge (Kendal circuit) is in Lancashire, as is Hawkshead (Ambleside circuit); and that the following stations which belong to circuits based outside Westmorland are located within our county: Temple Sowerby (Kirkoswald circuit); Glenridding, Shap, Cliburn, Morland, Newby, Great Strickland, Sleagill, Tirril, Helton, Bampton Grange (Penrith circuit); and Fell End (Sedbergh circuit). All of which has made our attempt to measure the strength of Methodism in the *county* a hazardous undertaking. Two illustrations will make the point clear. We have estimated the Methodist membership at Hawkshead for 1900, and deducted it from the Ambleside circuit figure for that year, since Hawkshead is not within our purview. Again, in the absence of statistics for the United Methodist Free Churches for 1900 we have made an estimate in the light of the decline in membership shown between the available Appleby circuit figures for 1909 and 1932. We have no reason to suppose that our estimated figures are wildly inaccurate (nor do we wish unduly to emphasise statistics), and we are confident that the small errors which almost certainly exist will not adversely affect the broad conclusions we wish to draw. The Quakers present nothing like the same difficulty, for although the Westmorland General Meeting embraces meetings over the boundary of Westmorland, membership returns for individual meetings are comparatively easy to trace.

We may now leave introductory considerations and proceed to our synoptic account of Westmorland nonconformity.

II – ORIGINS

Dr. Henry Cadbury has said that 'A movement like Quakerism is an emergence rather than a single datable act . . .'[1] The same may be said of all the Christian bodies we are to consider, and in this realisation there resides both a warning and a temptation. On the one hand we must not anachronistically read back our contemporary knowledge of the several denominations, with their relatively stable boundaries, into past ages. On the other hand, we must beware of thinking so narrowly in terms of *selected* recurrent themes that we overlook differences. An illustration will clarify this latter point. Acting under the impulse to demostrate the New Testament origins and subsequent continuity of their own denominations some older historians tended to fall into the trap we are noting with the result that, for example, Tertullian finds himself on the same church membership roll as John Smyth since both questioned paedobaptism.[2] With these considerations in mind we may now attend to the earliest tradition we have uncovered regarding Westmorland nonconformity.

It is said that there were baptists at Musgrave near Brough in the thirteenth century.[3] They lived in constant fear of persecution, and in order that their enemies might not trace their footprints in the snow, they waded along Swindale beck to their place of meeting. Kent surmises that the congregation in question may have been a product of the labours of the Wycliff preachers or of their successors. The Revd. Mr. Laurie, sometime Vicar of Musgrave claimed to have evidence to show that the tradition was factually based. We should dearly love to have access to it. Regrettably, we are not on firm ground until we come to the middle years of the seventeenth century.

The year 1640 found the English ecclesiastical establishment in a parlous state. The resources of Charles I had been seriously depleted by war with the Scots, and he was forced to convoke Parliament in November. This Parliament became known as the Long Parliament, notable for its undermining of the Anglican establishment by removing those High Commissioners who had governed the Church since Elizabeth's day; for impeaching twelve bishops; and for introducing bills for the abolition of episcopacy. On 22nd August 1642 Charles took up arms against Parliament.

Meanwhile the 'Gentry, Ministers, and Commonality of the Barony of Kendall' had presented a well-received petition to the House of Commons on 6th August. They expressed their loyalty, and their hope that further moves would be made towards 'a happy and thorough Reformation' and towards the punishment of offenders against the state.[4] On 18th November 1642 Parliament exhorted the inhabitants of the northern counties to prepare for their own defence in view of the presence in their midst of 'Papists and other ill-affected and malignant persons'.

With a view to enlisting the support of the Scots, Parliament sought to inaugurate an assembly to be charged with the responsibility of prescribing the government and worship of the church. After offering the King five bills, all of which proved unacceptable to him, Parliament drafted a sixth in June 1643. This found the monarch's favour, not least because to the 121 English divines were added 10 Lords and 20 commoners. Provision was also made for the inclusion of 5 ministerial and 3 lay commissioners from Scotland, and for 3 scribes. No Baptist representatives were proposed, and but 5 ministerial and 3 lay Independents. The predominance of Presbyterians would ensure an outcome consonant with the aspirations of the majority of Scots. The work of the Westminster Assembly began on 1st July 1643. On 17th August the General Assembly of the Church of Scotland formally adopted the Solemn League and Covenant, and the Westminster divines followed suit on 25th September. Among the objectives here were the defence of Presbyterianism in Scotland, the reform of the Church of England, and the maintenance of the King's legitimate rights.

The Westminster Assembly's *Directory for the Public*

Worship of God was authorised by both houses of Parliament on 4th January 1645. It was to replace the *Book of Common Prayer.* Penalties for continuing to use the latter, and for refusing to use the former, were introduced on 26th August 1645. In the same month the Assembly's *The Form of Presbyterial Church Government* was legalised, and thus presbyterianism became the established ecclesiastical polity, though as we have already indicated, it was incompletely applied to the country at large, and to Westmorland in particular. The Assembly was further instructed to produce a puritan revision of the Thirty-Nine Articles, but this work was set aside on the adoption of the Solemn League and Covenant, since the latter presupposed uniformity of doctrine as between England and Scotland. On 12th October Parliament ordered the writing of a new confession of faith, and on 4th December 1646 the Westminster Confession was completed. After revisions it was approved by the General Assembly of the Church of Scotland on 27th August 1647, and by Parliament on 20th June 1648. The Assembly's Larger and Shorter Catechisms were completed in 1647 and approved by Parliament on 15th September 1648. The Assembly met for the last time on 22nd February 1649.

Throughout this period Parliament was attempting to secure an adequate ministry. On 22nd November 1643 the Committee for Scandalous Ministers was set up and charged with the responsibility of purging the ministry of its less desirable members. In connection with the work of this Committee we may endorse Nightingale's judgement that 'there is no reason whatever to think that where the Clergy faithfully did their duty, and where they did not make themselves obnoxious to the Government, they were disturbed'.[5] Thus, Richard Archer of Windermere and William Richardson of Brough, both disaffected non-covenanters, were not removed from their livings, whilst Lancelot Lowther of Kirkby Thore was removed because of his pluralism, and not on grounds of nonconformity.[6] Evidence of a measure of compassion on the part of the sequestrators is provided by the case of William Cole[7] of Kirkby Lonsdale. On 17th August 1643 Parliament passed an ordinance under which one fifth of a sequestered living was to be given to the wife and any children of the sequestered minister. On refusing to give the wife of his predecessor, George Buchanan, one fifth of his living, Cole was informed that unless he complied with the ordinance he would himself be removed from the living.[8] Notwithstanding the measure of tolerance and compassion they possessed, the Westmorland Committee for Sequestrations had none too easy a time. On 10th August 1647 they were captured and imprisoned by a mob led by Anthony Knipe, and including Miles Halhead, who was later to become a Quaker. It is further testimony to the weakness of local presbyterianism both that the mobsters went unpunished, and that the local Sequestrations Committee was speedily reinforced by the addition of six Lancastrian esquires and gentlemen.[9] It remains only to add that the Committee for Scandalous Ministers was replaced by the Plundered Ministers' Committee, a body which, from February 1652/3 incorporated the Committee for the Reformation of the Universities (1646), and which in 1653 was itself replaced by the Trustees for Maintenance of Ministers. In turn this body was superseded from 20th March 1654 by Cromwell's Triers – or the Commissioners for Approbation of Public Preachers, to give them their official title.[10]

On 23rd April 1645 Parliament provided for a well-affected minister, approved by the Assembly of Divines, to be appointed to Appleby on a stipend of £150 p.a. In the same year Parliament began a review of local classical developments, and in the following year Westmorland announced its plans.[11] It was proposed to establish two classes, one for the Barony of Kendal, the other for 'the bottome of Westmerland Division'. The lists show the names of ministers and elders. Eight ministers are shown within the Kendal classis, of whom the following three have the clearest Presbyterian sympathies:

a Henry Masy.[12] He was appointed Lecturer at Kirkby Lonsdale on 6th August 1642, and was instituted to the living at Kendal on 14th November 1646. His name heads the list of those in the Kendal classis. Originally a staunch Presbyterian, he later revised his attitude towards Cromwell and took the Engagement on 20th January 1650. He appears to have died before 1653.

b William Cole. He was appointed minister of Kirkby Lonsdale in 1645, and remained there until c.1652. An opponent of the Quakers, in 1652/3 he joined Francis Higginson[13] of Kirkby Stephen in witnessing against James Nayler[14] at his trial at Appleby – of which more anon. Cole was ejected from Preston, but afterwards conformed.[15]

c Samuel Cole,[16] William's brother. He was minister at Heversham in 1646, and left there c.1650. He proceeded to Wybonbury, Cheshire, and thence to Duffield, Derbyshire. Though he does not appear on Calamy's list, he was silenced at the latter place at the Restoration.

The list for the bottom of Westmorland Division shows 23 ministers, and in three cases we have positive evidence of Presbyterian sympathies: Thomas Dodson of Ravenstonedale, George Fothergill of Orton, and John Dalton of Shap. We shall have cause to refer to these again, since they were the only three in the county in 1645 who were still there at the time of the 1660–62 ejectments. This classis list also includes the staunch noncomformist Matthew Wilkinson, who ministered at Bampton from 1641–9, and whose local good connections appear to have protected him at the Restoration.[17] That there were but 6 ministers with known and definite Presbyterian sympathies out of 31, as against 13 who are variously described as pluralists, non-covenanters and disaffected, malignants, unable, is a further indication of the difficulty of securing Presbyterian polity in Westmorland.

In August 1647 the army's General and Council submitted some 'Heads of Proposals' principally designed to remove penalties under the Conventicle Acts. These proved unacceptable to the monarch, and civil war flared up once more. On this occasion the Scots, in the interests of conformity along Presbyterian lines, supported the King – and both were roundly defeated. Parliament was made subservient to the will of the people, and prominent Presbyterians were removed from it. No longer was Parliament permitted to legislate in matters respecting religious practice. On 20th December 1649 the northern counties addressed a plea to Parliament for improved ministerial supply, and on 1st March

1649/50 a bill was passed to facilitate the settlement of ministers in those counties. At this point we may note in passing that although Cromwell's troops included many Baptists, they did not provide the inspiration for church planting in Westmorland that they did in neighbouring Cumberland.[18]

'The Agreement of the Associated Ministers and Churches of the Counties of Cumberland and Westmorland' which was published on 12th August 1656 bears the names of no known Westmorland signatories. For all that it made for such a degree of fellowship between both Presbyterians and Independents that it constituted in itself a bulwark against monopolistic presbyterianism. Nor, in our view, does it read like a thoroughly presbyterian document – though this is a disputed issue. Of Associations in general Nightingale has said that 'They were purely voluntary Associations, care being taken to make it perfectly plain that no real jurisdiction could be exercised over any one of the Associated Churches'.[19] On the other hand, and with particular reference to the Cumberland and Westmorland Agreement, Colligan mentions instances of oversight which 'suffice to prove that the Association was more than a federation and that it had internal executive power'.[20] Our own reading of the Agreement, however, suggests that the joining of the Association was voluntary; that its major emphasis was ministerial rather than magisterial; and that whilst members were under certain *moral* obligations to each other, the absence of sanctions, penalty clauses and the like suggests that Colligan's phrase 'executive power' is too strong – especially since the Agreement itself declares that 'we differ as to the power of associated Churches over particular congregations . . .'[21] The Agreement, whose architect was the Congregationalist Richard Gilpin,[22] is generally eirenic in temper, the one exception being its references to the Quakers. The authors and subscribers of the Agreement were quite plainly irritated at having to devote so much of their attention to these disturbing agents. With hindsight we may say that what was their misfortune is our privilege.

Paradoxically, Westmorland was among the least likely and the more likely of counties to provide fertile soil for the growth of Quakerism. Least likely, because of its strong Royalist associations, as represented by such men as Squire Duckett of Grayrigg and Sir Daniel Fleming[23] of Rydal Hall; and most likely because the ground had been well prepared by the activity and witness of the Seekers who, under their leaders Thomas Taylor, Francis Howgill and John Audland,[24] were centred in Preston Patrick, but drawn from Sedbergh, Yealand, Kellet, Kendal, Grayrigg, Underbarrow and Hutton.[25] In addition, there was that stimulus to radicalism provided by the general, social, educational and ecclesiastical neglect of the area.[26]

The presence of the Seekers explains the fact that Quaker-like experiences were known in Westmorland before, as George Fox claims, the name 'Quaker' was first bestowed upon the Friends by Justice Bennet of Derby on 30th October 1650, 'because we bid them tremble at the word of God . . .'[27] But however Quaker-like the experiences of some earlier Westmorland separatists may have been, Fox roundly declares that 'The Truth sprang up first in . . . Westmorland in 1652'.[28] This date coincides with his first visit to the county, but that Fox did not arrogantly emphasise the fact is suggested by the cordial reception he received from the Seekers.[29] They were, indeed, the 'great people in white raiment by a river's side [i.e. the Lune] coming to the Lord' of Fox's Pendle Hill vision;[30] and his meetings with them on 6th and 9th June 1652 at Sedbergh, 13th June at Firbank, and 16th June at Preston Patrick were to prove of crucial importance in the formation of the Society of Friends.

It appears that by the time of Fox's arrival in the county Thomas Taylor, the erstwhile leader of the Preston Patrick Seekers, had moved over to Swaledale, Yorkshire. For a time the Seeker community in this latter dale had shared his services with their brethren at Preston Patrick: indeed for a few months from February 1651 they contributed towards Taylor's stipend at the rate of £20 per annum. But Taylor, who in 1650 had been involved with three other ministers in a controversy in Kendal Parish Church on the question of the propriety of infant baptism, which at that time he opposed, resumed the practice to the dismay of the Preston Patrick Seekers. They found the sprinklings too *outward*;

thus Taylor transferred his ministrations entirely to Swaledale.[31] It was, as Rufus Jones declares, the 'convincement' to Quakerism of the remaining Preston Patrick leaders, Francis Howgill of Grayrigg and John Audland of Crosslands, that 'proved the turning of the tide for that cause, and opened the way for its great spread through England'.[32]

The Seekers already knew of that humble waiting upon the Lord so characteristic of Quakerism. They were already accustomed to meeting monthly at Preston Patrick for their General Meeting for mutual edification.[33] But in their quest of primitive Christianity they had, perhaps, fastened too much upon the letter, and had lost the spirit. Howgill himself said as much in his tract, *A Lamentation for the Scattered Tribes* (1656). The Seeker leaders were quick to recognise that Fox could supply their need. Howgill, after hearing Fox's oration by the tree in Sedbergh churchyard, concluded, 'This man speaks with authority and not as the scribes'.[34] On the following Sunday, Fox delivered a three-hour address to a crowd of over one thousand outside Firbank Chapel. Some were puzzled that he should preach in the open air,[35] but the impact he made was such that the rock from which he preached is to this day known as Fox's Pulpit.[36] Fox proceeded to John Audland's home at Crosslands, and while there he put John Story's offered pipe to his mouth, lest the lad should think 'I had not unity with the creation'.[37]

Fox moved on to Preston Patrick Chapel. Here he attended the General Meeting – an occasion never to be forgotten by Thomas Camm, then a boy of twelve years of age, and later the author from prison of *The Memory of the Righteous Revived* (1689). His parents, John and Mabel, were to join those Publishers of Truth who toured the world for the gospel's sake.[38] On Fox went to Kendal, where he preached in the town hall, and where 'one Cocks met me in the street and would have given me a roll of tobacco . . . , I accepted his love, but denied it'.[39] Kendal produced four of the Valiant Sixty: Christopher Atkinson, who later defected; Elizabeth Fletcher, who served in Dublin and Cork; and Thomas and Elizabeth Holme, who evangelised in South Wales. Miles Bateman's house at Underbarrow was Fox's next stopping place, and here he entered into controversy with many, including Edward Burrough.[40] Burrough, originally an Anglican, then a Presbyterian, ultimately became a follower of Fox, and died in London's Newgate gaol in 1662. In Fox's testimony to Burrough in the latter's *Works* the leader described his friend as being one 'who never turned his back on the Truth, nor his back from any out of the Truth'.[41] In addition to Burrough and to Miles Bateman himself, five other Underbarrow men joined the ranks of the Valiant Sixty: Miles Barrow, Miles Birkett, Miles Halhead, and Miles and Stephen Hubbersty. A 'great meeting' was held at the chapel at Underbarrow. Many residents of that place and of nearby Crook were convinced, as was James Dickinson of Crosthwaite. Apparently it was all too much for the 'priest' of the parish, for he 'fled away'.[42]

'Priest' William Lampitt of Ulverston (d. 1677) was among those who at this time sought to turn the people against Fox. Fox met the disenchanted at James Dickinson's home, and so successfully met their objections that Lampitt 'clearly lost the best of his hearers and followers and they came to see his deceit and to forsake him'.[43] Further successful meetings followed at Kendal on market day, and at Miles Bateman's house. Among the more influential shortly to be convinced was Thomas Taylor. It was at Judge Fell's house[44] that Fox first met him. In response to Fox's question Taylor confessed that 'he had never heard the voice of God nor Christ, to send him to any people, but he spoke his experiences, and the experiences of the saints and preached that . . .'[45] On his convincement Taylor resigned his living and became an itinerant. He was imprisoned for two years (1653–5) for preaching in Appleby church, and was again in Appleby gaol for a year from August 1657. Later imprisonments followed, and he died in Stafford gaol on 18th March 1682. His brother Christopher[46] was also convinced, and also served a two-year term of imprisonment at Appleby. His offence was disputing in the churchyard at Appleby with the vicar, Ambrose Rowlands, on the question of pluralities. From gaol he wrote *A Warning to the Nation* (1655) and *The Whirlwind of the Lord* (1655; reprinted 1656). He later opened a school at Waltham Abbey, Essex.

Towards the end of 1652 Fox was in Westmorland once

more. Some men armed with pikes and staves lay in wait for him but 'lighted on some Friends and missed me'.[47] The ambush party later arrived at Fox's meeting, but were foiled once more – this time by the presence of the recently convinced Justice Gervase Benson[48] and 'many considerable people'. Grayrigg[49] was among Fox's next calls: it is a village rich in Quaker associations. Here he stayed at the home of Alexander Dixon, Thursgill, and met the Baptist 'priest' Richard Stookes, who was confounded by the Lord's power.[50] Francis Howgill was born at Todthorne, Grayrigg, and buried at Sunny Bank, the home of Captain Henry Ward. It was at Ward's home that George Whitehead[51] of Orton, then aged sixteen, attended his first Quaker meeting in 1652. Later in the same year he heard Fox preach in the same house, was convinced, and subsequently became one of the Valiant Sixty, dying in 1723.

It used to be thought that Fox himself did not visit Ravenstonedale. Nicholls, however, provides some contrary evidence which suggests that in 1652 Fox, John Blaykling of Draw Well, Thomas Robertson of Grayrigg, and several others evangelised the dale. John Pinder and James Clarkson received the preachers into their homes. It was from the Ravenstonedale meeting that John Fothergill (d. 25th June 1665) set off on his mission to London and elsewhere; and it was here that Richard Pinder of Wath was convinced in 1652. In 1657 he began a ministry which took him to various parts of England and Scotland, and also to many places overseas including America, Barbados, Bermuda and Jamaica. Fox was followed into the district by James Nayler, who preached at the homes of Robert Shaw of Orton, John Pinder of Ravenstonedale, and John Knewstub of Mallerstang.[52] In November both Nayler and Howgill were arrested at Mallerstang, at the instigation of Francis Higginson. They were brought before Justice Burton at Higginson's own house at Kirkby Stephen, and then taken to Appleby gaol, where they remained from 24th November 1652 until the following Easter sessions.[53] Meanwhile the 'priests' of Lancaster were enraged by Fox, and petitions were drawn up in Lancashire and Westmorland the object of which was to seek the suppression of Quakerism. In the event they were not sent to

Parliament on grounds of cost. Fox, however, was arrested and tried at Lancaster on 18th October. All of which episodes were described in a volume to which Fox and others contributed entitled, *Saul's Errand to Damascus, with His Packet of Letters from the High Priests against the Disciples of the Lord, etc.* (1653).[54]

Francis Higginson reacted swiftly to *Saul's Errand* in his *A Brief Relation of the Irreligion of the Northern Quakers* (1653), a work which was later (incorrectly) described as 'the first book that ever was written against that Sink of Blasphemies'.[55] Higginson, a man of Presbyterian persuasion, was instituted at Kirkby Stephen on 27th October 1648, 'though probably he had already been here some time'.[56] His anti-Quaker tract recounts the arrival in the area of Fox and his friends – 'Satan's seeds-men' – and amounts to a castigation of them under several headings: 'Of the horrid blasphemies of the Quakers against God and his Christ; Of the erroneous opinions of the Quakers; Of the wicked practices of the Quakers [i.e. their meetings, speakings, quakings, fastings and railings]; Of their idleness, savage incivilities, and their irreligious, bloody, barbarous, and turbulent practices'. Among specific points criticised are groanings and grovellings which are reminiscent of epilepsy; public nakedness; shouting at justices; heterodoxy regarding the atonement; opposition to the sacraments; the wearing of hats during worship, and so on. As for railings: 'The Billingsgate oyster women are not comparable to them'. More than once Higginson likens the Quakers to the Munster anabaptists.

At a meeting at Arnside in 1653 Fox healed the paralysed arm of Richard Myers. Sadly, Myers refused to obey the Lord's summons to proclaim a message in York, and he died within a year.[57] Fox was shortly to be found in the north of the county, at Strickland Head. Here he addressed a large meeting which included Justice Henry Draper of Durham, and 'many contenders'. Fox records that 'The priests and magistrates were in a great rage against me in Westmorland and had a warrant to apprehend me, which they renewed from time to time for a long time, yet the Lord did not suffer them to serve it upon me'.[58]

In May 1653 John Gilpin was, as he claimed, deluded by

the Kendal Quakers and possessed by the devil. In July he published a pamphlet to prove it, and to document his happy deliverance.[59] A further hostile tract noted that eight cases of Quaker public nakedness were reported in the years 1653–4 at Kendal, Hutton and Kirkby Stephen.[60] Howgill and Nayler sought to answer such charges in a pamphlet entitled, *A woe against the magistrates, priests, and people of Kendal . . . Also the stumbling-block removed from weak minds, who are offended at the strange signs and wonders acted by the servants of the Lord scornfully called Quakers in the northern parts of this nation.*[61] Howgill defends nakedness as being prophetically symbolic of the fact that the magistrates' 'covering is now rent, and your garment is to be torn'. For his part, Nayler contends that 'the Lord has caused some of his servants to go naked along your streets, as in *Kendal* and *Kirkby-Stephen,* as figures of his wrath to come upon that pride and fulness that Priests and people live in'. Concerning the methods of their opponents, Howgill rhetorically asks, 'what God is this ye serv that must be defended with clubs, swords, Rulers and carnal weapons . . .?'.

In 1654 William Cole of Kirkby Lonsdale entered the fray and published a pamphlet against the Quakers entitled, *The Perfect Pharisee, etc.* This drew a reply from James Nayler, published in May of the same year, and headed, *An Answer to the Books called The Perfect Pharisee, etc.* Among the Quakers' most persistent clerical opponents was William Brownsword, Vicar of Kendal from 1658–1672/3.[62] A Presbyterian in Cromwell's day, Brownsword subsequently conformed and threw in his lot wholeheartedly with the Royalist cause. His anti-Quaker pamphlet, written in November 1659 and published the following year, is adequately described by its title: *The Quaker-Jesuite or, Popery in Quakerisme: Being a clear Discovery 1. That their Doctrines, with their Proofs and Arguments, are fecht out of the Council of Trent, Bellarmine, and others. 2. That their Practises are fecht out of the Rules and Practises of Popish Monks. With a serious Admonition to the Quakers, to consider their ways, and return from whence they are fallen.* The Quaker Thomas Story retaliated in his 1660 pamphlet, *Babilon's Defence Broken Down, etc.* For our final illustration of churchly invective we return to the 'cheerfully subscribed' Agreement of the Cumberland and Westmorland ministers. They attribute the Quaker presence in their area to the fact that 'Satan is enraged' and hence 'he disgorgeth from his hateful stomach a swarm of Quakers; these . . . come upon us like a furious Torrent . . .'.[63]

Both Quakers and their royalist arch-opponents suffered under Cromwellian rule. Thus, on the one hand, Taylor points out that 'Quakers were punished under the Blasphemy Act of 1650, the Act of 1656 requiring persons supposed to be Roman Catholics to take an oath abjuring the Papal authority, the Vagrancy Act of Elizabeth, the Lord's Day Act of 1656, and for the refusal to pay honour to magistrates'.[64] In all 3,170 Friends suffered for conscientious reasons prior to the Restoration.[65] On the other hand, those corporation officials at Appleby who refused to promulgate Cromwell's directions, were punished by a special charter of restrictions; and Major-General Lambert was notably efficient in the matter of the sequestration of Royalist land and funds.[66]

Turning for a moment to relatively unsensational matters, we find that the Quakers were soon making arrangements for that great missionary enterprise in which so many of them were to engage. The Valiant Sixty were sent out in 1654, and Margaret Fell herself kept the accounts from 1654–7 of a fund collected at Kendal 'for the service of truth'.[67] More domestically, the Kendal Friends bought a graveyard, (extant) known as the Sepulchre, on Fellside. They paid Robert Baccus £2 for it in 1656, and had it walled by Robert Barrow and his men.[68] Following a General Meeting held at Scalehouse near Skipton in 1658, forty Friends, including three from Westmorland, signed an order advocating that a collection be taken for overseas work. In the event £252/11/8 was realised.[69] At the Kendal Monthly Meeting for Lancashire, Westmorland and Cumberland held on 8th July 1659 arrangements for the recording of births, marriages and deaths were put in hand.[70] But Quakers were never more assiduous than when recording their sufferings, as we shall shortly see.

Reverting to George Fox, we find that in 1657, having escaped the magistrates in Kendal, he came to Strickland once more, and on this occasion he addressed a quiet gathering of gentry at a race meeting.[71] In 1660 he was at Arnside for a General Meeting of Westmorland and Cumberland Friends,[72] and he was in the same place for the same purpose again in 1663. Then, after passing through Underbarrow, Grayrigg, and Sedbergh, he visited Strickland Head once more. After a 'precious' meeting on the common he made his escape into Northumberland from the 'wicked justices' who were searching for him.[73] Among his numerous enemies at this time were Sir Philip Musgrave and Sir Daniel Fleming, to both of whom the Restoration had given an increase of power. Fox continued into Cumberland, and on his return journey stayed with Gervase Benson, who told him that Fleming had offered five pounds to any man who could apprehend Fox. But once again Fox was spared.[74] The founder of the Quakers left Westmorland for the last time in March 1680, bound for London.[75]

On 3rd September 1658, Oliver Cromwell died. Following his death the army became increasingly prone to internal friction, and the country at large came to feel ever more intensely the need of change. On 29th May 1660, Charles II came to the throne, and the Bishops, deprived of office since 1646, swept back into power. Charles had signed the Declaration of Breda on 4th April, thereby declaring 'a liberty to tender consciences; and that no man shall be disquieted, or called in question, for differences of opinion in matters of religion which do not distrub the peace of the kingdom . . .'. Many ministers, however, became increasingly restless under the well-founded suspicion that Charles would not adhere to the Declaration. We thus enter that complicated period of ministerial resignations on principle, out of fear, or under pressure; and of ejectment. Following the passing of the Convention Parliament's Act of 1660, under which sequestered ministers were restorable to their livings, many ministers all over the land began either to conform or to resign. The Act received the eager support of Richard Sterne and Guy Carleton, Bishop and Dean of Carlisle respectively,[76] and of Royalists in general. On 15th April 1661 the King convened the Savoy Conference in the hope of eliminating religious friction; but it was a forlorn hope, and the

Conference disbanded on 24th July. By that date the Convention Parliament had already been replaced by an ultra-Royalist successor, among whose leading lights was Edward Hyde, Earl of Clarendon,[77] who gave his name to that series of laws, the Clarendon Code, which so greatly oppressed dissenters. This Code comprised the following Acts of Parliament:

a The Corporation Act, 1661, which prohibited nonconformists from holding office in civil corporations;

b The Conventicle Act, 1664, which decreed that if five or more persons (other than members of the same household) over the age of sixteen met for religious purposes they were liable to a fine of £5; and to transportation to a colony other than Virginia or New England for a third offence;

c The Five Mile Act, 1665, which was designed to prevent nonconformist ministers and teachers from residing within five miles of any corporate town, or of the place where they had formerly been employed.

To these must be added the Act of Uniformity of 1662, which required all ministers of religion and schoolmasters to give their 'unfeigned assent and consent' to the contents of the *Book of Common Prayer*. Many were to suffer under this severe legislation, and mere statistics tell but little of the number and the names of those ministers who left their livings in Westmorland between 1660–62. Our tentative conclusion is that they may be classified under three headings, as follows:[78]

1 *Ministers who left their livings prior to 1662, or during 1662:*

a James Greenwood. He was admitted curate of Old Hutton on 6th September 1654. We have no evidence to support either the *pro* or the *con* of his epitaph: 'He was much liked as a preacher, but was accused of some things that were scandalous, by which his memory is blackened.'

b Christopher Jackson. He was Rector of Crosby Garrett (otherwise referred to as Crosby-on-the-Hill) by 1657.

Of him we read that 'Some ministers who had conformed, once telling him that he had a bare coat, he made this answer, "If his coat was bare, it was not turned." ' The sequestered incumbent was restored to Crosby Garrett by June 1661.

c Christopher Langhorne, Vicar of Askham. He was here in June 1660. Foster's *Alumni Oxonienses* appears to err in giving 1662 as the date of his ejection. As Nightingale shows, he was at Askham as late as June 1660. Lancelot Harrison, the sequestered Vicar, was restored to the living by August 1661.

d Timothy Roberts. He was admitted Vicar of Barton on 14th November 1655.

2 *Ministers ejected in 1662:*

a Francis Higginson, Vicar of Kirkby Stephen, who subsequently conformed. He was admitted on 26th October 1648.

b John Wallace (or Wallis), curate of Killington, sometime of Heversham. He is said to have been 'a man of the same description' as Greenwood, but this is more cryptic than informative.

3 *Ministers concerning whom there are doubts:*

a Gabriel Camelford of Staveley. He is not listed by Calamy under 'Westmorland'. Nightingale in *LN* appears to follow Samuel Palmer's *The Nonconformist's Memorial* (1803) in placing him within our county, though Palmer does locate 'Stavely' on the borders of Lancashire. Nightingale seems to think in terms of the Staveley to the north of Kendal, and the root error is that Palmer has Camelford in the wrong county. Nicholson and Axon demonstrate conclusively in *ONK* that it was from Staveley in Cartmel, Lancashire, that Camelford was ejected.

b John Dalton, Vicar of Shap. He was here in 1645, and is given as one who afterwards conformed. But Nightingale shows that his ejection cannot conclusively be proved.

c Thomas Dodson, curate of Ravenstonedale from 1628. Calamy states that he afterwards conformed, but Nightingale shows that his ministry at Ravenstonedale was continuous until his death in 1673. There is no evidence either that he was ejected, or that he subsequently conformed. It may be that the patronage of Philip Lord Wharton was responsible for his security of tenure.

d George Fothergill, Vicar of Orton. Calamy and Palmer deem him to be an after-conformist, but he was still at Orton in May 1663, and had subscribed on 22nd August 1662.

e John Smith, Vicar of Kirkby Lonsdale. Nightingale shows that since he left Kirkby Lonsdale before the end of 1657, he could not have been ejected therefrom.

It thus appears that six Westmorland ministers were definitely ejected between the years 1660 and 1662. Of these one, Higginson, subsequently conformed. Discounting Camelford, the maximum possible number of ministers ejected in the county is ten, and they are the same ten whose names appear in A. G. Matthews's *Calamy Revised.* We are therefore at a loss to understand on what grounds Matthews, in a table in the introduction to his book,[79] gives a total of fourteen ejected ministers under 'Westmorland', of whom two subsequently conformed. What is quite clear is that none of the eight Baptists ejected in England between 1660–1662 was of Westmorland.[80]

The upshot is that although, during the Commonwealth, there had been a number of Independent and Presbyterian ministers of ability in the county, after the Restoration leaders of these persuasions were few. Some, like Higginson, conformed, or did not allow themselves to reach ejection. Others, such as James Greenwood, lived out their days in obscurity. The Independent Jeremiah Marsden, who came as Lecturer to Kendal in 1658, remained for nine months only.[81] Some of the most powerful and acceptable preachers of the day, including Francis Howgill and John Audland, had, as we have seen, become first Seekers and then Quakers. If we discount Gabriel Camelford's disputed connection with

Crook, the only ejected minister whose name is associated with any of Westmorland's early dissenting congregations is Christopher Jackson; and even in his case the link is more tenuous than has sometimes been supposed. On ejection he removed to the neighbourhood of Ravenstonedale, and under the protective wing of Lord Wharton.[82] The latter, as well as endowing his famous Bible Charity, was later to provide an endowment of £100 p.a. to the dissenting cause at Ravenstonedale.

Clarendon remained in power until 1667, in which year he had to flee for his life to France. His legislation remained in force, however. Indeed, in 1670 the Conventicle Act was not only renewed but strengthened. At last, on 15th March 1672 Charles issued his Declaration of Indulgence, under which both buildings and preachers – whether itinerant or resident – could be licensed. The Declaration remained in force only until 7th February 1673. On principle no Quakers availed themselves of its privileges; as it happens no Baptist licences were taken out in Westmorland. As we shall see, the county boasted but ten licences, two for teachers and eight for householders, all of them almost certainly for Presbyterians, and all in the Kendal area.[83] The licences were withdrawn on 3rd February 1676, and thereafter the number of presentments for nonconformity increased.[84] Meanwhile, in 1673 the Test Act had been passed. Though intended to debar Roman Catholics in particular from holding government offices, this Act constituted a further restriction of the rights of all nonconformists, whether protestant or catholic. How did the Westmorland dissenters fare during these stormy years, and to what extent had they established themselves by the end of the century?

We consider first the principal town, Kendal.[85] Although Brownsword conformed, a Presbyterian Thomas Whitehead[86] and an Independent George Benson,[87] ejected from Dalton and Bridekirk respectively, shortly moved into the district and began to conduct house services. The nonconformist cause received great encouragement when Richard Frankland[88] came to nearby Natland. Educated at Giggleswick Grammar School and Christ's College, Cambridge, he was ejected from St. Andrews, Auckland, Co. Durham in

1662 because he would not confess, either privately or publicly, the invalidity of his non-episcopal ordination. He retired to his native Rathmell; in 1670 he began an academy there, and in 1672 he took out a licence to teach. He removed to Natland in 1674 'upon a call from a Christian society there'. He preached at various places in the neighbourhood, and trained a total of 304 men for the ministry and for the legal and medical professions. Frankland was assisted by John Issot,[89] by his own son Richard, and by John Owen. Lectures were delivered in Latin and encompassed logic, metaphysics, somatology, pneumatology, natural philosophy, divinity and chronology. His students were permitted to graduate from the Scottish universities after spending only one session north of the border. Discipline at the academy was strict, and there is evidence that not all students were happy there.

Among visitors to Natland were Oliver Heywood the Presbyterian,[90] and Thomas Jollie, the Independent.[91] The former's son John, and the latter's son Timothy[92] were among Frankland's students. Friction arose between Jollie and Frankland over the question of ordination, the former favouring the Independent practice or ordaining men in the church which had called them. But in 1682 they both shared in an ordination, and in November 1692 they both declined to take part in the ordination of David Crossley, a Baptist.[93] In 1681 Frankland was excommunicated for his part in the first nonconformist ordination in Yorkshire – that of John Issot on 10th July 1678. His friends secured the cancellation of the order. In 1683 he had to leave Natland under the provisions of the Five Mile Act. He took his academy to Calton Hall, Yorkshire, and then in 1684 returned to Dawson Fold, Westmorland. In 1685 he proceeded to Hart Barrow near Cartmel, Lancashire, and before November 1686, to Attercliffe, Sheffield. In July 1689 he returned to Rathmell, leaving Timothy Jollie in charge of the Attercliffe academy.[94] On 2nd February 1691 Frankland was again excommunicated for not answering a citation to Archbishop Lamplugh's court.[95] On this occasion Lord Wharton and Sir Thomas Rokeby intervened and secured an absolution from the Archbishop at King William III's command. In 1695 Frankland was again indicted, but the indictment was quashed on 10th February. Brought before the spiritual court in 1697, his case was postponed at Michaelmas on the order of the Archbishop. Difficulties notwithstanding, Frankland continued to teach until his death on 1st October 1698. Although permitted freely to preach after the passing of the Toleration Act of 1689, his academy had ever been under threat.

Frankland was by no means the only Westmorland dissenter to suffer under the Clarendon Code. Nicholson and Axon list a number of Kendalians whose names appear in the Kendal Indictment Book for 1669–91, as having been fined for assembling for nonconforming worship under the reinforced Conventicle Act of 11th May 1670. To Daniel Fleming this Act was 'very moderate'. In a letter to Williamson he reported that 'Wee have convicted many Quakers', but he was, we may suppose, somewhat discomfited by the Independents: 'Our Independents keep close and are cunning, they not exceeding the number mentioned in the Act. And after wee have rooted all conventicles, the levying of 12d for every Sunday will I hope bring them to church. It is as clear as the day that nothing will convince them of their errors so soon as the drawing of money from them . . .'[96] But Fleming spoke too soon. In 1672 the houses of John Garnett, George Benson, William Syll and James Atkinson were licensed in Kendal town; and further licences were granted to the houses of James Cock, Kendal Park, William Warriner, Whinfell, and John Hind and Edward Bridges, both of Heversham.[97] At the same time Thomas Whitehead and George Benson became licensed preachers. Again, on 13th January 1698/9 the houses of Thomas Ellery, Applethwaite, and John Hind, Stainton, were licensed for worship.[98]

Although the Baptists do not seem to have been organised in the county at this time, they may claim a female martyr, as the following inscription in St. Oswald's, Ravenstonedale, makes plain: 'To the glory of God, and in memory of Mrs. [Elizabeth] Gaunt, daughter of Anthony Fothergill, Brownber. She was the last female martyr burnt at Tyburn for the cause of protestant religion Oct. 4, 1685.'[99] Mrs. Gaunt kept a tallow chandler's shop, and although a poor woman, she financed the escape of Burton to Amsterdam after the Rye

House Plot. He returned to England with Monmouth, and after the defeat at Sedgemoor he escaped to London. As Hume has it,

> 'One of the rebels, knowing her humane disposition, had recourse to her in his distress, and was concealed by her. Hearing of the proclamation which offered an indemnity and reward to such as discovered criminals, he betrayed his benefactress, and bore evidence against her. He received a pardon as a recompense for his treachery, she was burned alive for her charity.'[100]

Mrs. Gaunt was shortly to be eulogised in verse, probably not his best, by Benjamin Keach.[101] He speaks to her

> 'Who wast condemn'd a cruel death to die,
> 'Cause thou relievedst men in misery . . .'[102]

As for the dissenting causes which were established in the county in the seventeenth century, we find that Ravenstonedale[103] claims that with the longest continuous life. A persistent tradition affirms Christopher Jackson's connection with the (nominally Presbyterian) church there. In *LN* Nightingale follows Calamy in upholding this tradition, and the list of ministers provided by P. L. Woodger and S. E. Hunter is headed by 'Christopher Jackson, B.A., 1662–1689'. But as Nightingale showed later in *ECW*, whereas Jackson may well have preached in the area, his name does not appear in the Conventicle Returns for 1669, the Presentment Lists for 1670, or the list of Indulgence Licences for 1672. He grants, however, that the protection of Lord Wharton may have rendered the licensing of Jackson unnecessary, and he affords register evidence to show that Jackson definitely resided in the district. He married a local woman, Annas Taylor on 7th April 1664, and he was buried at Crosby Garrett on 29th May 1689.

Next, the old foundations at Stainton and Crook.[104] As we have seen, in 1672 two licences, both for Presbyterians, were taken out for houses in Heversham parish. It seems likely that one of these was for Milnthorpe and the other for Stainton. We recall too that on 13th January 1698/9 John Hind's house at Stainton was licensed. Work on a chapel was begun at Stainton in 1697, and it was opened for worship in

1698. In the meantime the Returns for 1691 speak of a meeting '5 miles W. of Kendall'. This is most likely to refer to Moss Side, Crosthwaite, the house of James Garnett, which was registered on 15th January 1691/2. It is possible that this may have been the forerunner of the cause at Crook, where a chapel, no trace of which now remains, was erected in the late seventeenth century.

Stainton chapel (now U.R.C.).

Finally, from the first entry in the (now) Unitarian Baptismal Register, we learn that there was an organised Presbyterian congregation in Kendal in 1687. This congregation (significantly enough) invited the *Independent* Thomas Jollie to become their pastor, but he declined. A call was then addressed to James Hulme,[105] who ministered from c.1687 until his death at the age of 58 in 1688. William Dearnley was minister in 1690, and had left Kendal by early 1692; and a Mr. Thorneley of Kendal was allowed £6 p.a. by the Presbyterian Fund in 1699/1700.[106]

We turn now to the post-Restoration fortunes of the Quakers. At the time of Captain Robert Atkinson's abortive Kaber Rigg Plot of October 1663, the Quakers as a body were under great suspicion. The object of the Plot, with which the authorities had been conversant since July, was to force the King to act upon his promises made at Breda, especially that regarding the granting of liberty of conscience to all except Romanists. Sir Philip Musgrave was convinced of Quaker involvement in the Plot. Although Atkinson himself was not a Friend, it appears that at least one, Richard Fawcett of Ravenstonedale, who had already been *disowned* by the Quakers, joined him; and certainly Thomas Braithwaite of Burnside who was at that time, or shortly afterwards, a Friend, assisted in Atkinson's escape to York. Atkinson was eventually caught and hanged, probably at Appleby, in 1664.[107]

The extant materials for the period with which we are concerned deal largely with Quaker sufferings and organisation. Autobiographies abound, as do tracts, both devotional and polemical. We must content ourselves with the briefest mention of some such matters as far as they pertain to Westmorland.

The following examples from Besse's *Sufferings* will indicate something of the extent and type of Quaker sufferings:

> 1663: 'On the 19th of *October*, fifteen Friends were taken at a Meeting in the House of Widow *Cocke*, at Birkhagge, for which they were afterward indicted at the Sessions, and several of them fined. Three of them, *John Ayrey, Robert Barrow*, and *Brian Lancaster*, were committed to Prison, where they lay above eleven months.'
>
> 1664: 'In or about this Year, many were fined for their religious Meetings, and committed either to the Common Gaol, or House of Correction, for one, two, or three Months, and some of them longer, *viz . . . Elizabeth Morland* . . . who, while in the House of Correction, had a young Child sucking at her Breast . . . *Katharine Clark*, a married Woman, with a sucking Child . . . *Mary Holme*, a Women then great with Child . . .'

For the years 1670 and 1671 Besse provides a long list of those who were proceeded against under the Second Conventicle Act, and among other more trivial offences which earned disproportionate penalties are the following:

> 1675: 'In the Year 1675, *Joseph Baines, John Hodgson*, and *John Yeates*, all of *Killington*, were prosecuted for *Easter Offerings*, and the said *John Hodgson* also suffered Imprisonment for Tithes at *Kendal*, thirteen Weeks, for a

trivial Claim of two Lambs, and about six Fleeces of Wool'

Further evidence of local Quaker sufferings may be seen in a folio volume of the Westmorland Quarterly Meeting, which has been described by Ernest E. Taylor.[108] The book is inscribed as follows:

> 'In this Booke is Recorded the Sufferings of Frds in Kendall Quary Meeting wch at p'sent is kept by me JN WILSON
>
> Kendll ye 28th 1st mo. 1716'.

The sufferings are listed under four headings: tithes; meetings; refusal to swear; and absence from public worship. It appears that of all the local Quakers Thomas Camm suffered more than anyone else. Between 1668 and 1699 he was distrained upon no fewer than 33 times. His offences were mainly under the heading of the non-payment of tithes, and in all he forfeited £62/12/8. Taylor observes, 'a striking witness is borne to his strict integrity by the fact that in 1681 he was liberated from prison on promising "to return when sent for" '.[109] Taylor further remarks upon the irony of history by which in 1677 25 Quakers within the Barony of Kendal were charged with being 'Popish recusants'. Also charged were four 'papists' including none other than Anthony, son of Squire Duckett of Grayrigg, the Quakers' old enemy.[110]

On 9th November 1686 the Earl of Rochester addressed a letter from the Treasury Chambers to Sir Daniel Fleming, who had expressed to Thomas Camm of Cammsgill his desire to show leniency to the Quakers if it were the King's will. Rochester's advice was that the King's pleasure is 'not to have these poore people so troubled upon the account of their being Quakers only. If, therefore, you find no other complaints against them, you will be pleased to show them what kindness you can.'[111] Thus Besse was able to close his account of Quaker sufferings in Westmorland with a reference to the year 1690. From 1681 to 1690, he informs us, goods to the value of £359/16/5 had been taken from Friends for non-payment of tithes. That there were still occasional moves against Quakers is clear from a document submitted to both Houses of Parliament entitled, *A Brief Account of many of the Prosecutions of the People call'd Quakers in the Exchequer, Ecclesiastical, and other Courts etc.* (1736).[112] There are here recorded seven cases in Westmorland of suits to recover tithes between the years 1696 and 1718.

Remarkably, the Friends not only survived, but increased under persecution. What to Sir Henry Bennet was an irritating refusal on the part of Quakers to 'abate . . . of their obstinacy'[113] was to them the stalwart maintenance of the cause of truth.

As if external oppression were not enough for them to contend with, we hear of occasional internal disputes amongst the Friends. By far the most serious of these was the Wilkinson–Story separation.[114] John Wilkinson of Millholme, New Hutton, and John Story of Goosegreene, Preston Patrick, were among the early Publishers of Truth. At some time after they returned from Wiltshire they separated from Fox and Margaret Fell. The complicated issues centred in the question of individual *versus* group discipline, Underbarrow, Preston Patrick and Hutton being the meetings most affected. One cause of friction was the persistence of the Preston Patrick Friends in meeting secretly out of doors during a time of persecution under the Conventicle Act. The Kendal Minutes of 3rd February 1674 record a request that John Blaykling and Thomas Robertson ask the Preston Friends 'whether they did not beleeve that there was a weaknesse in them for meeting without doores in the time of the informers or not, and that answeres be brought in to the next quarterly meeting . . .'. The Quarterly Meeting of 2nd May 1675 received the reply from Preston, and judged that some of their brethren *had* been guilty of weakness, and invited those concerned to acknowledge the same at the next Quarterly Meeting. The separation which resulted from friction of this kind was widespread and long-lived, especially in Westmorland where it originated. By 1709, however, remaining separatists were few in number, and many of them had deviated greatly from Quaker moral discipline.[115]

Internal and external difficulties notwithstanding, the Friends made progress. In 1675 one of their oldest meeting houses, that at Brigflatts, near Sedbergh, Yorkshire, was erected. The Kendal Minutes record a decision of 2nd February 1675 to the effect that because of their worth Fox's papers and epistles be recorded in the Minute Book and read in every particular meeting.[116] On 6th August 1682 Robert Barrow was able to write to Fox: 'Well blessed be the Lord, our meetings is as large as ever & truth prospers hitherto because of which the adversaryes thereof begins to be angrye, swell & breake forth now of late in our countye more then of late years.'[117] But the Toleration Act of 1689 was not far distant, and as we have already seen, persecutions were shortly to diminish in number. On 1st May 1687 it was proposed to build a meeting house at Kendal, and in the following year the building was opened.[118] On 5th May 1688 the Friends of the Strickland Monthly Meeting recorded a collection of £3/9/0 towards the Kendal Meeting House Fund.[119] In the wake of the Toleration Act of 1689 seventeen farmhouses were licensed for Quaker worship within an eleven mile radius of Sedbergh.[120]

As well as witnessing, writing, suffering and squabbling, the Quakers gave themselves to educating, and their activities under this last heading are of special interest. Pioneering educational work was done in Westmorland – initially as the outcome of local initiative, and later in response to corporately bestowed advice.[121]

George Whitehead, born at Sunbiggin, Orton, was already teaching at his home village when he was convinced by the repentance of a young maid under the preaching of Thomas Arey in 1652. In 1654 he left Westmorland for an itinerating ministry, as described in his posthumous *Christian Progress of George Whitehead* (1725). There is no evidence that he confined his schoolmasterly attentions to Quaker children after his convincement. For his part, Thomas Taylor did not begin to teach until he resigned his living on convincement in 1652. Supreme among the early Quaker schoolmasters in the county, however, was Thomas Lawson.[122]

A brilliant classical scholar, Lawson was educated at Cambridge. He was also said to be the most noted herbalist in England. Convinced by Fox of the unlawfulness of preaching for hire in 1653, he resigned his living at Rampside,

Lancashire, and though never a Quaker preacher, he served ably as clerk to the Monthly Meetings. He was frequently distrained upon for non-payment of tithes, and in reduced circumstances he appealed to Margaret Fell for money from the general fund for the purchase of books. She herself employed him to teach her daughters botany and herbal medicine. On 24th March 1658 Lawson married Frances Wilkinson, and they settled at Great Strickland, where he kept a school. His was one of the longest lived of early Quaker schools. It was still in existence at the time of the Episcopal Visitation of 1673;[123] and in a letter to Fox written from Great Strickland and dated 20th February 1689 Lawson writes, 'I follow my ancient employment of schooling . . .'.[124] It appears that by 1691 Lawson was free of local educational responsibilities, for William Meade wrote to him in that year inviting him to come as tutor to his son and his cousin.[125] Lawson's death, however, prevented the fulfilment of this request. A monument erected by a former pupil at Lawson's grave at Newby Head stands there to this day.[126]

That Thomas Lawson's concern for the underprivileged was acute is shown by his *An Appeal to the Parliament concerning the Poor, that there may not be a beggar in England* (1660),[127] in which he advocated the cause of basic education for all. This was a theme later taken up by Friends on a semi-official basis. The Yearly Meeting of 1688 gave some attention to education, but did not propose the establishment of separate Quaker schools. By 1690, however, much clearer advice was being given to parents, who are now exhorted 'not to send [their children] to such schools where they are taught the corrupt ways, manners, fashions, and languages of the world, and of the heathen in their authors, and names of the heathenish gods and goddesses; tending greatly to corrupt and alienate the kinds of children into an averseness or opposition against the truth, and the simplicity of it . . .'. But still schools were thought of as being the concern of individuals. The 1695 Yearly Meeting, however, laid it as an obligation upon meetings 'to see that schools, and schoolmasters, who are faithful Friends, and well qualified, be placed, and encouraged, in all counties, cities, great towns, or places where there may be need'.

Westmorland was among the first counties to respond to this advice. On 3rd November 1695 an attempt was made by the local Quarterly Meeting to secure the services of Christopher Winn as schoolmaster:

> 'This meetting having had under their consideration ye erecting of A scooll for ye education of their children and have Agreed yt Kendall may be ye place for one yeare, J. Blayklinge is desired speedily to write to Christr Win and give him account of what is here Agreed upon, and yt £16 per Ann be assured to ye Scooll Master.'

This initiative failed, but at length a school was opened in Stramongate in January 1698, on the same financial terms, under John Jopson.[128] The school flourished, and in 1706 an assistant master was appointed at £10 p.a. Thus began an educational venture which was to survive with only one term's break (the summer term of 1899) until well into the twentieth century.

It remains only to indicate the strength and spread of Quakerism in the county. Braithwaite estimates that in 1661 there were between 30,000 and 40,000 Friends in the country at large[129] – a comment to be read in the light of the fact that the population of the country in 1688 was about 5½ millions, of whom but 800,000 lived in the province of York. Westmorland's share of the Quaker membership was proportionately large, both because the Seekers so readily threw in their lot with Fox, and because of Quaker success in attracting to their fold dissenters of other theological hues. Three Quaker conventicles were reported in the Conventicle Returns compiled at the request of Sheldon, Archbishop of Canterbury, in 1669, and these were the only conventicles returned for the county. They were all in the Kendal deanery, at Grisemere, Bolton and Burton, and their attenders numbered approximately 80, 40 and 50 respectively.[130] In 1688 the Kendal and Strickland Monthly Meetings were established as constituents of the Westmorland Quarterly Meeting.

George Fox died in 1691, and it is thought that by that date Quakers were the largest nonconformist group in the land.[131] One of the Kendal records for that year shows that local Quakers applied for eight 'meeting places for religious worship' at the houses of John Thirnbeck and Isabell Ward, Middleton; Edmund Garnett, Barbon; John Hodgson, Berkeside; Joseph Baines sen. and jun., James Baines, and Samuel Parrot, Killington. A new meeting house was erected at Preston Patrick in 1691 for the congregation as reunited after the Wilkinson – Story controversy, and another meeting house was erected at Burton in Kendal in the same year. It was restored in 1876, but is now closed. Of the meetings noted in this chapter (and excluding Yorkshire's Brigflatts), only that at Kendal survives with a continuous history from the seventeenth century.[132]

III – THE EIGHTEENTH CENTURY

By 1699 the Kendal dissenting congregation was in receipt of aid from the Presbyterian Fund, and by 1702 William Pendlebury was pastor to the flock.[1] Trained under both Frankland, and Chorlton of Manchester,[2] he arrived in Kendal in 1701, and was ordained, together with some others, at Warrington on 16th June 1702. It was he who opened the Kendal baptismal register, and in 1706 his sole publication appeared: *The practical influences of the speculative doctrine of Christianity demonstrated. In a Discourse upon I Tim. vi. 3.* Pendlebury was succeeded by Samuel Audland[3] who, since he was related to the Independent minister John Audland, and since he did not receive a grant from the Presbyterian Fund, may well have been himself an Independent. An interregnum followed Audland's death on 24th October 1714, and then, in 1716, Caleb Rotheram became pastor.[4] He was ordained during the following year, probably in August.

A native of Great Salkeld (b. 7th March 1694), Rotheram's academic lineage is as follows: John Chorlton of Manchester academy was a pupil of Richard Frankland; Thomas Dixon[5] (a native of Ravenstonedale) studied under Chorlton; and Caleb Rotheram attended Dixon's academy at Whitehaven. During his ministry, in 1720, the Market Place chapel was erected, and as for his congregation: Evans's *List of Dissenting Congregations and Ministers in England and Wales, 1715–29* records a Presbyterian congregation of 205 hearers. Of these, 15 had votes, 10 were gentry, and the remainder were yeomen and traders. In answer to a question put to the Kendal Churchwardens on the occasion of the Archdeacon's Visitation of 1717 they replied, 'Thers but two meetings of Dessenters in our Town the one of Presbeterians, the other of Quakers. We do not know whether their meeting houses are licensed or no, the Presbeterian Ministers name is Mr. Rodderham.'

Market Place Presbyterian (now Unitarian) chapel, Kendal.

Dr. Dixon died in 1729, and Caleb Rotheram opened his Kendal academy in 1733, whilst continuing as pastor of the church. In all, about 120 laymen and 56 ordinands were trained under him, among the most illustrious of the latter being George Walker, F.R.S. (1735–1807),[6] the Arian minister who was to serve at both Warrington academy and Manchester college. On 27th May 1743 Rotheram was admitted to the degree of M.A. Edinburgh, and at once proceeded to his D.D., which was awarded after he had publicly defended a thesis he had written within the field of the Evidences of the Christian Religion. This thesis, his only publication, appeared in print later in the same year under the title, *Dissertatio . . . de Religionis Christianae Evidentia, &c.* In it he refuted the view of Locke, Tindal and Evanson 'that the probability of facts depending on human testimony, must gradually lessen in proportion to the distance of the time when they happened, and at last become entirely evanescent'.[7] Above all, Rotheram loved science and mathematics, and for an additional fee he would introduce his students to the higher reaches of the latter discipline. After an illness, during which he left his academy in the charge of his Calvinistic assistant, Richard Simpson, Rotheram died on 8th June 1752. His funeral sermon was preached on 14th June by one of his ex-students, the Revd. James Daye, of Lancaster. This sermon, entitled *The Christian's service compleated with honour* was subsequently published. Rotheram's academy continued for a few months under Simpson, and then closed.

Caleb Rotheram's third son, also Caleb, was ordained and inducted as successor to his father (the doctrinal suspicions of some notwithstanding) on 26th August 1756.[8] Both father and son valued freedom of thought, though the latter appears to have been more unorthodox than the former. Nevertheless, over the fifty years ending in 1773 the number of dissenters in Kendal remained in the region of 200. In 1781, through the mediation of Dr. Priestley,[9] Rotheram travelled to Montrose to baptize the children of William Christie,[10] one of the founders of Unitarianism in Scotland, who at the time was suffering socially on account of his beliefs.[11] In 1792 Rotheram took a leading part in a public meeting held in Kendal to protest against the African slave trade. It was probably he who drafted the resolution which was presented to Parliament by the county member, Sir Michael le Fleming.[12] The dissenters were by no means so keen to be associated with a resolution passed at a meeting in the Moot Hall on 14th December 1792. This took the form of a declaration of loyalty to the government in the face of the likes of Tom Paine (who, though not named in the text was very much in the minds of those who drafted it), and of a request to the magistrates not to grant licenses to any innkeeper who permitted seditious meetings to be held on his premises. A fortnight later Rotheram's congregation met for its annual meeting, and composed a much more restrained document in which they not only expressed their loyalty to the government and their disapproval of seditious meetings, but also their confidence in the 'wisdom of the Legislature to remedy any defects which may be in the best form of government . . .'[13] Just over three years later, on 30th January 1796, the younger Rotheram died aged 63, having completed the longest ministry in the history of his chapel. He was buried in the chapel yard.

During the ministry of the Rotherams the Provincial Meeting of Cumberland and Westmorland was in operation. Its first known meeting was held at Brampton on 10th August 1709, and its last probably at Penrith in August 1785.[14] In 1791 the national Unitarian Society was formed, and among its founder members were Rotheram and Dr. Henry Ainslie.[15] By the time of Rotheram's successor, John

Harrison,[16] who served from 1796 until his death at the age of 72 on 6th May 1833, the Market Place congregation had become decidedly unitarian in doctrine. (Nicholson and Axon point out that at the time of the building of the chapel, even if the founders were not *anti*-trinitarian, they were not test-imposing trinitarians).[17]

Meanwhile, in April 1763, thirty-one orthodox dissenters from Kendal and district had approached the Associate (Anti-Burgher) Presbytery of Edinburgh, 'praying that ministers might be sent from Scotland to preach the Gospel in Kendal'.[18] Since the names of those concerned in this petition do not survive we cannot be certain that any of them were members of the Market Street chapel; but it is possible that at least some of them were. A chapel was built on Beast Banks for the new congregation, and James McQuhae was ordained to be their minister in 1764. Presumably in 1771 (the Tockholes Church Book informing us that he was minister *there* in that year) McQuhae took part in the ordination service of an Independent minister, thereby incurring the displeasure of his Synod. He informed his congregation that he had now embraced the Independent position, and a division resulted. Some members, especially James Smith, a prominent elder, objected to McQuhae's continuing as minister, and shortly pastor and supporters took their leave. In 1774 Thomas Simpson was ordained to the ministry and inducted to the Scotch chapel, but by 1780 the congregation could no longer maintain his stipend. The cause decreased in strength, employing such supplies as were available, until 1806, when the chapel was sold. A loan of £100 from Abraham Williamson of Keswick enabled the congregation to retrieve the chapel, but in 1812 it was finally surrendered.

For a time McQuhae's supporters worshipped in 'The Fold', Stricklandgate, and then, in 1779, George Burder came upon the scene'[19] Burder was ordained at Lancaster on 29th October 1778, James McQuhae (who had removed from Tockholes to Blackburn in 1777) sharing in the service.[20] During his Lancaster ministry Burder preached at numerous places in Westmorland, including Kirkby Lonsdale and Kendal. Indeed, on leaving Lancaster in 1783 he wrote, 'My principal usefulness, I apprehend, was in being instrumental in introducing the gospel, or assisting in introducing it, in Kendal, Bootle, Garstang, Preston, and some other places'.[21] It was on 9th June 1779 that Burder met the Revd. Daniel Gibbons of Ulverston[22] in Kendal. 'We took an old playhouse for one year; in which, in the course of the following month, I preached for the first time.'[23] At length the Kendal congregation was able to occupy its own chapel in New Street (later, Lowther Street), and Burder could write on 12th September 1781: 'The Lord having greatly prospered our attempts at Kendal, a new and spacious chapel, capable of seating about 400 persons, without galleries, was opened this day, to my great joy. Mr. Gibbons preached in the morning, I in the afternoon, and Mr. Hunt in the evening'.[24] The church was allowed £100 as being their share of the property of the Scotch chapel, and it is an engaging ecumenical note that this sum, borrowed by the Presbyterian remnant from an Anglican incumbent, Wilson, was employed towards the erection of the new Independent chapel. James Kenworthy,[25] ordained on 16th August 1783, was the first minister at Lowther Street, and the cause made its last appearance in *CYB* in 1928.

That the congregations of Crook, Stainton and Kendal were thought of in relation to each other is suggested by a passage in Frankland's will of 1698, in which he made provision for two sermons to be preached annually in May by 'wise sober and virtuous learned men'. One sermon was to be delivered at Stainton, Kendal or Crook, and the other at Attercliffe or Rathmell. The preaching fee was to be 6/8d per sermon. John Atkinson was minister at Crook in the early eighteenth century. He was followed by a Mr. Stevenson, and he by Samuel Bourn. Bourn embraced Arianism in 1719, and left Crook in 1720. By the time Evans compiled his List there was a congregation of 130 including one voter. The work gradually declined, so that on 3rd March 1745–6 the managers of the Presbyterian Fund transferred the allowance 'formerly made to Crook and Harborough' to Mr. Blackburn, minister at Ravenstonedale, 'till the congregation at Crook and Harborough revive'. This it did not appear to do, and a mid-century date for its extinction is almost certainly correct.

The first known minister at Stainton was John Atkinson,

not to be confused with his namesake at Crook. He was at Stainton in 1708 (whereas the Crook Atkinson removed to Cockermouth in 1701), and was still there in 1726. In 1722 he replied to a sermon, preached in 1719 by Joseph Dodson of Penruddock and later printed, entitled, 'Moderation and Charity'. To Atkinson this constituted a sad denial of Trinitarian doctrine, and his reply was entitled, *Jesus Christ the Son, essentially the same with God the Father.*[26] Atkinson was succeded by John Kirkpatrick, and he by James Scott the Berwickshire man, who came down to England from Edinburgh where he had studied, because he had heard of the dearth of ministers in the south. He settled at Stainton in 1739, and left for Horton in Craven in 1741. In 1750 he moved to Tockholes, and thence to Heckmondwike in 1754. He here maintained a pastorate and an academy, and is especially remembered for having, through his academy, kept back 'the wave of Socinianism which a century ago swept especially northern England.'[27] Evans's List gives Stainton 130 hearers and (astoundingly and almost certainly erroneously) 86 voters. But decline followed. The Thompson mss. inform us that in 1772 'the congregation at Stainton is reduced very low by the decay of some families and the removal of others. Their numbers do not exceed 30 or 40.' And after visiting the place on 21st November 1779 George Burder referred to the cause as 'an old meeting . . . almost deserted'.[28] Stainton later revived and continues to this day.

The first pastor of whose formal association with the Ravenstonedale cause we have proof is Timothy Puncheon, who was trained under Richard Frankland at Attercliffe. The Presbyterian Fund Minutes of 8th June 1691 record an allowance of £5 to Puncheon, the minister at Ravenstonedale. He was followed by James Mitchell, who was in charge in 1697. The fortunes of the cause fluctuated, and during the ministry of John Magee (appointed 1713–4) a secession took place. The disaffected seem to have enjoyed the support of Dr. Dixon of Whitehaven, himself a former member of the Ravenstonedale meeting, and the cause of the friction was presumably doctrinal. Colligan holds that Crippen and Dale are anachronistic in suggesting that the seceders were motivated by Arianism. His own view is that the dispute was between Arminians and Calvinists. But, as Dr. Nuttall has shown, 'Arminian' is yet another of those ambiguous terms by which it is our lot to be confronted, and that the earlier, non-missionary-minded 'Arminianism of the head' *did* cause many General Baptist causes, and others too, to veer towards Arianism, and thence in the direction of that Unitarianism in which so many of them ended.[29] The Ravenstonedale seceders were served by Caleb Rotheram, who remained with them for about a year prior to his removal to Kendal. James Malleson followed him, but the cessation of financial aid from the Presbyterian Fund in 1723 seems to have brought the cessation to an end. According to Evans's List the Ravenstonedale Presbyterians had a minister, but the number of hearers is not stated; whilst the Independents had 300 hearers, 3 voters and 4 gentry – most of the congregation being tenants of Lord Wharton. Magee remained with the main body until 1732, and during his ministry the present chapel was erected in 1726, and registered at Appleby on 10th April 1727. A period of litigation ensued concerning Magee's successor, James Ritchie, who was suspect because of his reservations concerning the 1647 Confession of Faith.[30] By 1753 he was an Arian. During this period Magee gave oversight until his death in 1743.

The High Chapel, Ravenstonedale (now U.R.C.).

Nicolson and Burn (1777) record the presence of 59 dissenting families in Ravenstonedale, but by the 1780's the Independent congregation, like others in the county, had declined in strength. A new lease of life was granted with James Hill's arrival on the scene in 1790.

To what may the eighteenth century decline of the old rural dissenting causes be attributed? Certainly the sensational, one-word answer, 'Unitarianism' will not do. Whilst Bourn at Crook *may* have disturbed his flock with his incipient personal Arianism, there is no evidence that he did so, and every indication that he left the village as soon as his new beliefs were firmly rooted. At Stainton John Atkinson was a staunch trinitarian, and Ravenstonedale's doctrinal secession was short-lived. Moreover, not only were the rural congregations comparatively isolated from those *avant garde* currents of thought which undoubtedly *did* modify the theological complexion of many town churches, their ministers – especially Scott and his progeny – were generally fairly firmly in the Calvinistic tradition. Again, *the* church in urban Kendal which did become unitarian did *not* decline during the period in question: as we have seen, its membership remained in the region of 200 for many years. Nor is there any evidence to suggest that an unduly rigid doctrinal orthodoxy proved to be the stifling agent in the rural areas. Finally, as we shall shortly see, the Inghamites, those harbingers of Revival in the county, do not appear to have had meetings in Stainton, Crook or Ravenstonedale, and it is therefore unlikely that rural Independents were siphoned off to livelier pastures. It is most probable that the disadvantages of geographical isolation, the death and removal of some members, and the loss of zeal of others, were the major factors in the decline.

The Independents were not the only nonconformists to have their troubles in eighteenth century Westmorland. With the advent of the century we leave the period of great Quaker enthusiasm, and enter an era in which Friends became increasingly preoccupied with organisational problems and Christian discipline. The general result of this was the cramping of that very inwardness which Friends at their best have ever sought. For evidence of a changing spirit we may refer to a letter written by Samuel Bownas to James Wilson on 12th February 1751.[31] Bownas, born in Westmorland c.1676 writes:

> 'It seems to me (and I have been a minister 54 years) that I had more service, and better success in my ministry, the first 20 years, than I have since had for a long time. I do not find any fruit or good effect from what I do that way; and yet what I am concerned in seems to be very acceptable and well received by others; but they don't, to my observation have that good effect, as I could desire they should. I have closely examined what the fault is, but don't find it out.'

Again, he continues, whereas now the hearers will say, 'The man spoke well', in the past 'I rarely went a journey but I found some convincement . . .' No doubt the changing socio-political climate following the passing of the Toleration Act of 1689 had something to do with the diminution of Quaker zeal. After a period of persecution, during which only the most determined stayed the course, Friends tended to settle down to the enjoyment of their new-found comparative security. Indeed, the Epistle of the 1689 Yearly Meeting positively encouraged them to be 'as the Lord's hidden ones, that are always quiet in the land . . .'. In a word, the Quakers were approaching what has been called their 'age of Quietism': not indeed that this phrase should be taken as implying that *all* Friends *entirely* withdrew from the world and into themselves. Their school at Kendal continued – we shall have cause to refer to this later, and also to the enlivening effect of the visit of John Woolman to Westmorland in 1772. Nor does the phrase imply utter silence! On the contrary, especially in the early part of the century, Quakers made noisy and hostile forays into the theological arena, assaulted the views of others, and received as good as they gave: and all this despite the 1689 Epistle's exhortation to keep out of 'all airy discourses and words'. One example will suffice. In 1708 John Atkinson, who by now had left Crook for Cockermouth, replied to a Quaker pamphlet entitled *Absolute Predestination not Scriptural.* Atkinson's volume is entitled, *A discourse of election, showing the nature, the proof, the properties, the improvement of election, to which is added, A vindication of this doctrine of election.*[32] Happily, Quakers and other dissenters were more constructively employed later in the century in their common opposition to the slave trade, and in their advocacy of social reform.

References to Baptists in Westmorland continue to be few and far between in the eighteenth century. We hear of some members of Samuel Bourn's congregation at Crook (c.1711) who objected to paedobaptism. Bourn respected their views to the extent of devising a service of infant dedication, though a number of his own children are entered in the Kendal baptismal register.[33] In 1726 John Sedgfield, who ministered at Tottlebank, Lancashire, for over forty years,[34] preached a sermon in Kendal which was afterwards printed under the title: *Jehovah Tsidkenu: or, a discourse on that glorious title of Jesus Christ, the Lord our Righteousness.*[35] The sermon was a defence of the imputed righteousness of Christ at a time 'when revealed Religion is become Matter of Contempt and Ridicule among many of the learned Part of the World . . . '. There is no reason to suppose that this was Sedgfield's only visit to Kendal. Finally, there were three Baptists among Dr. Rotheram's students at Kendal:[36] George Braithwaite (1736), Daniel Noble (1747),[37] and John Wiche (1739). We may assume that since all but one of the Westmorland churches of Old Dissent were in the doldrums by the third quarter of the century, the same is true *a fortiori* of any less well grounded Baptist movements. Solid educational work, and the fidelity of such men as Atkinson and Sedgfield notwithstanding, the time was ripe for revival.

Two varieties of methodism – those associated with the names of Benjamin Ingham and George Whitefield – preceded Wesleyanism in Westmorland, and we shall look at each in turn. Whereas Whitefield's methodism was of the Calvinistic kind, Ingham's was influenced by Moravian piety. Benjamin Ingham[38] was born at Ossett on 11th June 1712, and whilst an undergraduate at The Queen's College, he joined the Holy Club. He was ordained by John Potter,[39] Bishop of Oxford, on 1st June 1735, and soon his evangelistic activities were carrying him over a wide area. For a time he served with Wesley in Georgia. On returning to England he itinerated in Yorkshire until, on 6th June 1739, he was forbidden by the Wakefield Visitation to preach in any of the churches in the diocese of York. He took to the road, and for many years covered up to two hundred miles per week. He preached in barns, farmhouses, and in the open air, and it was not long before his circuit extended from Nottinghamshire in the south to Durham and Cumberland in the north. Of Ingham Dr. Harrison wrote, 'His societies [in Yorkshire] should be regarded as the first fruits of Methodism in the north of England, although many of them were handed over later to the Moravians'.[40] If we are to understand the rise and fall of the Inghamites – which was exemplified in Westmorland as clearly as anywhere else – we must first attend to the doctrinal and ecclesiastical context of the movement.

Ingham's relationship with Wesley's Conference, which had first met in June 1744, was somewhat ambiguous. He became a Conference member at Leeds, but also held his own Conference as well. His Moravian inclinations were by no means shared by John Wesley who, as early as the summer of 1740, voiced his reservations concerning the Brethren. Wesley viewed with concern the passivity, and the tendency towards antinomianism, which he detected especially in those Moravians who had been influenced by Peter Molther. From the other side, neither the Moravian Count Zinzendorf nor Ingham himself was happy either with Wesley's doctrine of perfection, or with his emphasis upon discipline in the Christian life.[41] Thus when Ingham handed over his societies to the Moravians on 30th July 1742,[42] relations between himself and John Wesley became strained. In 1753, however, Ingham broke from the Moravians because he could not subscribe to Zinzendorf's policy of refraining from agressive evangelism in favour of the establishment of a few religious communities. He resumed the role of an itinerant preacher, and the question of Wesleyan – Inghamite union was raised at the Wesleyan Conference of 1753. The answer given was that 'We may now behave to him [i.e. Ingham] with all tenderness and love, and unite with him when he returns to the Old Methodist doctrine'. Two years later, at the Leeds Conference, the question was raised once more. The Countess of Huntingdon, whose sister-in-law, Lady Margaret Hastings,[43] Ingham had married on 12th November 1741, was eager that such a union should take place. She sent Whitefield to Newcastle upon Tyne to meet the Wesleys with a view to discussing the matter. Charles Wesley favoured union, but John did not – perhaps he feared that Inghamite 'occasionalism' as regards ecclesiastical discipline and order would make an ill match with his own clearly defined structure. It may also be that he detected early signs of that openness on Ingham's part to heterodox ideas which was shortly to wreak such havoc upon the Inghamite societies.

Inghamite internal difficulties arose acutely after Ingham had read John Glas's *The Testimony of the King of Martyrs concerning his Kingdom, John viii. 36, 37, explained and illustrated in Scripture Light* (1727 etc.) and Robert Sandeman's *Letters on Theron and Aspasio* (1757), which were published under the pseudonym, Palaemon.[44] So impressed was Ingham by these works that he sent two of his preachers, William Batty and James Allen, to Scotland.[45] The envoys met Sandeman in Edinburgh and Glas in Dundee, and Allen returned home converted to their opinions and practices. Among these was one forbidding fellowship with unbelievers. This was pressed to extremes by the Glasites in rather the same way, and with some of the same results, as by the Exclusive Brethren of latter days. It entailed the breaking of family ties in some cases, and the utter refusal to fraternise with those of other churches. Doctrinally, Sandeman's view of the work of Christ, namely that what justifies the sinner is simple assent to the truth of the apostolic testimony, apart altogether from any internal witness of his own soul, brought the giants – supremely Andrew Fuller – into battle. The effect of such teaching upon the Inghamite societies was traumatic. Ingham found that he could not follow Allen all the way, but since he lacked the organising genius of a John Wesley, there was little he could do to hold his fellowships together. The efforts of Whitefield, the Countess of Huntingdon and William Romaine notwithstanding, the Inghamite causes declined through controversy, and Ingham himself became a sick man. Some Inghamites seceded to form Glasite or Sandemanian churches under Allen's leadership, as we shall see.

Benjamin Ingham visited Kendal c.1740, and preached on a hill to the west of the town. In due course a plot of land, and a barn belonging to William Wilson were acquired by the society he gathered. In 1756 the barn was conveyed to William Batty, and converted into a chapel. It was known locally as the Pear Tree Chapel on account of a pear tree which stood in front of it until a storm blew the tree down in November 1821. Benjamin Ingham himself officiated at the first recorded baptism, that of Robert, son of Kendalians George and Dorothy Pearson, on 10th March 1756. Thomas Rowlandson of Grayrigg served as elder from 1762 – 9, when he resigned having espoused the views of Ingham's erstwhile colleague, James Allen. His successors in the eldership were Christopher Batty (1774 – 97) and William Wilson (1774 – 1804).

Inghamite chapel, Kendal.

Among those converted under Ingham were three ex-soldiers, Edmonson, Hunter and Brogden. Of these, Hunter founded the Inghamite cause at Kirkby Lonsdale – despite the opposition of incumbents Croft and Cock of Kirkby Lonsdale and Tunstall respectively.[46] Thompson recounts that on one occasion a mob, acting on Croft's instructions, attacked two of Ingham's preachers, and damaged nearby property, shouting, 'We want no vendors of new notions . . . Let us keep off the hereticks'. The preachers appealed to the magistrate, hinted strongly at their good connections with government (i.e. *via* Lady Huntingdon), and obtained redress, the repair of the damaged houses, and a license to preach at a house in Mitchelgate. Once more the mob intervened and captured the preacher. However, the intervention of James Ashton of Underley Hall, who had known the preacher at college, brought peace.[47] The Inghamites of Kirkby Lonsdale, and those of nearby Burton in Lonsdale, later followed James Allen. In July 1763 Allen recorded his opinion that there was 'the prospect of a little church' at Kirkby Lonsdale.[48] Eventually, however, numbers dwindled and the causes died out.

Kirkby Stephen, where on one occasion George Whitefield preached to over two thousand people, was also the scene of Inghamite labours. Here Mr. Brogden, though discharged from the army many years previously, was pressed for further service whilst preaching at an inn. After some days in prison locally he was taken to Newcastle, where he was confined for four months until released through the intervention of the Countess of Huntingdon. He lived to attain his century, and to see the Inghamite chapel built at Kirkby Stephen.[49] In time James Allen's influence led the Kirkby Stephen Inghamites towards the position of Glas and Sandeman, and in the 'account of his friends' written in July 1763 Allen was able to claim 10 men and 13 women at Kirkby Stephen; 15 men and women at Newby; and 4 men and 4 women at Gayle, Yorkshire – his home village. Allen died in 1804, 'unconnected with any other sect or party', and was buried in the meeting house graveyard at Gayle. Thompson aptly remarks: 'The writing of this story would have been easier had Allen's journal been handed down to posterity. He left it in his will to his third child, Oswald, exhorting him that after reading it the journal be destroyed as "it was fit for no one's personal use" '.[50]

Apart from that at Kendal, the most prominent Inghamite chapel in the county was at Birks near Warcop. Its influence extended across the north of the county from Stainmore to Shap. Among the more practical missionary steps taken by the Inghamites here was the erection of a footbridge over the Eden at Sandford for the convenience of their members who lived at Hilton and Murton. Birks chapel, owned by James Richardson, elder of the church, was probably built in 1757, and was registered with the Bishop of Carlisle in 1760. Ingham first visited it in the former year, and made his last entry in the baptismal register on 12th April 1763. This register, which also contains entries by Batty and Allen, records 121 baptisms in all. It opens with 'Jane the daughter of James and Ann Perkins of Greenside in Ravenstonedale, Baptized March the 4th 1757', and concludes with an entry made by the elder, Thomas Bell, on 30th October 1826. 53 burials are recorded, from 4th June 1758 (John Hill) to 29th January 1807 (William Robinson). The last minister at Birks was a Mr. Capper, who also kept a school.[51] In their hey-day the Inghamites also had meetings at Crosby Garrett, Asby, Grayrigg, and, as we shall see, at the home of Stephen Brunskill's father at Gaisgill.

Inghamite chapel (now a barn), Birks.

The effects of Ingham's work on Wesleyanism are interesting. We might have expected that just as George Fox found a ready-made audience in the Seekers, so John Wesley would find the nucleus of his societies in the Inghamites. Superficially, the opposite appears to have been the case. Thus, when the Revd. George Abbott, Chairman of the Wesleyan Methodist District, laid the foundation stone of Soulby chapel on 26th May 1892 he said,

> 'Methodism was longer taking root in Westmorland, than in almost any other part of England. Why? Was it because Wesley did not sympathise with the spiritual wants of the place? Not a bit of it, the ground was already occupied . . . The Inghamites had occupied it, and a mighty power for good they were.'[52]

There is some force in these remarks – and no doubt there

was a psychological difference between the Seekers who were consciously awaiting new light, and the Inghamites, who probably thought they already possessed it. And it is true that, for example, the influence of Birks Chapel and of the Kendal Inghamite cause, was powerful. On the other hand, however, we know of no Inghamite work in the Ambleside district. Yet, despite the fact that Wesley visited that town more than any other in the county – on ten occasions in all[53] – it was not until some sixty years following his last visit that a Wesleyan society became established there. Thus, if Inghamite success explains the late establishment of Wesleyanism in some places, the innate conservatism, irreligion or apathy of the people combine in various proportions to explain it in others. Further, James Wilson's judgement concerning Cumberland may well have some validity with respect to neighbouring Westmorland: 'it was only after Methodism had become an integral portion of nonconformity that its influence began to be felt in towns or country villages.'[54] Conversely, some of Ingham's success in Westmorland may have been due to the fact that he sat more lightly to things Anglican than did Wesley.

In another respect the Inghamites were of great assistance to Wesleyan advance in the county. Or, at least, out of Inghamite disarray sprang Wesleyan hope, and this largely in the persons of the Brunskills of Winton, to whom we shall shortly turn. We must first however, note that methodism with Calvinistic overtones which was ardently proclaimed in Westmorland by George Whitefield.

In a letter written from Rossendale, Lancashire, on 14th June 1750 Whitefield said, 'I am now going towards Kendal, then to Whitehaven'. Two days later he wrote to Lady Huntingdon from Newby Cote: 'I am now in Mr. I[ngham]'s circuit, and purpose being at Kendal next Thursday.' On 21st June he wrote from Kendal to the Rev. Mr. H[artley] as follows: 'This leaves me at Kendal, where I arrived this morning and where GOD willing, I shall preach the everlasting gospel this evening. An entrance is now made into Westmoreland; . . . at Kirby-Steven the people behaved exceedingly well.' On 26th June he was able to report his success to the Countess in these words:

'Such an entrance hath been made into Kendal, as could not have been expected. I preached twice to several thousands last week, and the people were so importunate, that I was prevailed on to return hither last night. The congregation was greatly increased, and the power of the Lord was displayed in the midst of them.'[55]

Not indeed that all was plain sailing, as the report in *Life and Times* makes plain:

'Mr. Whitefield preached on the brow of a hill, which overlooks the town, to many thousands of hearers. That night, some evil-disposed persons got into the barn and stable where his travelling carriage and horses were locked up: the leathers were all destroyed, and the carriage otherwise much abused: they also cut off the long tails of a pair of black horses that he had had a long time, and greatly esteemed. Nevertheless, he rejoiced at the success attending his labours.'[56]

Not all were as overjoyed by this success as was Whitefield himself. Thus, Curwen notes the following entry in the Tunstall Parish Church register: 'In the year 1751 the Methodists settled and established their doctrines at Kendal, which is a doctrine contrary to reason and scripture.'[57] The writer of this comment was echoing the sentiments of Richard Osbaldeston, Bishop of Carlisle, who in 1749 wrote the following letter to Richard Burn, then Vicar of Orton:[58]

It is a concern to me to hear the Methodists have made their progress into your Parish in this Diocese; the best measures as experience has hitherto shewn us, to prevent their infection from spreading, are to use great prudence and moderation in every step we take to defeat their attempts to disturb the minds of our people. Those by arguments drawn from reason and Scripture may be prevented from going astray, and the same applied with meekness and wisdom to enthusiasts will expose their errors tho' never convince them. The extravagant delusions and wild conceits they espouse leave no room for the impression of truth, but seem to entitle them to the pity and compassion shewn to the inhabitants of Moorfields. So far as they are like reasonable men, they have a right to all privileges the

Law will give them, but in my opinion I do not apprehend they come within the Toleration Act, that was made for the case of such Dissenters as were then in being, and can't in any fair construction be extended to those of other denominations that have since sprung up. I know the Methodists have had the benefit of that Act in a neighbouring Diocese, and had their house licensed, but when that was done I thought the measure wrong as I still do. I begin my journey this day for Yorkshire, therefore have not leisure to say more on the subject at present, but shall be glad to hear how matters go between you and the turbulent spirits you have to deal with, and shall be ready to give you any assistance in my power for the service of the Church.

Rose Castle Richd. Carlisle
Sept. 4th 1749.

One month later to the day, John Wesley first set foot in Westmorland. Mr. T. A. Bainbridge has extracted those passages from Wesley's *Journal* which refer to Westmorland,[59] and we may content ourselves with a brief summary of his findings.

Whilst on his way from Whitehaven to Leeds to meet Whitefield, Wesley stayed overnight at Old Hutton on 4th October 1749. The 12th April 1751 found him in Ambleside, and on 27th May 1752 he preached at Clifton 'to a civil people who looked just as if I had been talking "Greek" '. (II 228).[60] Wesley visited Kendal for the first time on 9th April 1753. Here he preached in a room formerly used by the Inghamites. The congregation sullenly refused to sing the first hymn, but after having been moved by the sermon, they joined heartily in the second. After the service the majority of those present accompanied Wesley to his inn. (II 250). On 25th June 1764 Wesley passed through Kendal once more *en route* to Keswick, and when he called again the following year, this time making for Liverpool, he could write, 'there is now a real work of God. The genuine gospel takes root, and sinners are converted to God.' (III 210). When Wesley was next in Kendal in 1767 he discovered that a great change had taken place: 'Seceders and mongrel Methodists have so surfeited the people here, that there is small prospect of doing good . . .' (III 322). We may not be too wide of the mark in understanding this as a reference to the Inghamite troubles. Wesley recorded one more visit to Kendal, in 1788, when he was eighty-five years of age. Bainbridge's table of the dates of Wesley's Westmorland visits is as follows:

Ambleside	1751 1753 1757 1768 1770 1772 1774 1781 1784
Clifton	1752
Kendal	1753 1761 1764 1767 1768 1788
Brough	1766 1768 1779
Appleby	1766 1768
Old Hutton	1749

Judge draws attention to the fact that Wesley's *Diary* provides evidence of a further visit to Ambleside, on Thursday 8th May, 1786.[61] Whilst Wesley's messages must have brought encouragement to many of his hearers, there are no records to show that any societies were established *immediately* following his visits. Inghamite disarray and local initiative were to take a hand.

The Brunskills of Winton were among those who became separated from the Inghamites. They sent a deputation to John Wesley, whose Conference was in session at Bristol. The emissaries made the arduous journey *via* York and London in three days, and were rewarded by Wesley's promise of help. Two Wesleyan evangelists, Jacob Rowell and Christopher Hopper, were working in Wensleydale, Swaledale, Teesdale and Weardale at the time, and Wesley urged them to cross Stainmore and go to Brunskill's at Winton, where they would be welcomed. So it was that the Brunskill's home became, for a period of forty years the focal point of Wesleyan activity in north Westmorland. In time the extensive Dales circuit extended from Hexham to Wensleydale, and westwards to Kendal, which town was served by the circuit's travelling preachers from 1791–4. For the next three years the Barnard Castle ministers paid fortnightly visits to Kendal. Then Lancaster ministers took over until 1805, in which year Kendal was raised to circuit status and given Thomas Gill and Thomas Biggins as ministers.

The firm establishment of Wesleyanism in Kendal and elsewhere owes much to another Brunskill: Stephen, of Orton.[62] He was born at Gaisgill Row on 5th November 1748. As he tells us in his autobiography:

> 'My parents at that time were members of the Established Church, but strangers to experimental religion. When I was about seven or eight years of age, Mr. Ingham, and the preachers in connexion with him, visited our neighbourhood. Many attended their preaching, which excited much interest and attention. They formed several societies, in which were to be found persons of the highest respectability. The fruit of their labours was a visible reformation among the people . . .'[63]

Stephen's father and brother were shortly converted, 'But I received no benefit; I still remained unconcerned about my soul, and a slave to sin'.[64] There follows a reference to the visit of Batty and Allen to Scotland, and Brunskill attributes Inghamite troubles to the effect of doctrines imported from Scotland which, he somewhat inaccurately states, 'were those of Calvinism'.[65] The erstwhile Inghamite preachers followed the new teachings, and refused to preach at the Brunskills' house any more, because Stephen's father 'continued to believe, and stedfastly to maintain, that Christ tasted death for every man'.[66] For the next ten years Brunskill senior sought to establish Wesleyanism in the area, but the nearest Wesleyan station was a dozen or more miles away, and 'the former professors of religion had rendered themselves so odious to the ungodly, by their contentions and loose morals, that scarcely any would come to hear'.[67] A providential escape from death during a severe snow storm notwithstanding, Stephen 'continued a stranger to God, seeking happiness in playing at cards, and in other foolish diversions, till the 24th year of my age'.[68]

Stephen was employed in the slating business, and with another young man travelled into Nottinghamshire, Lincolnshire, Derbyshire and Yorkshire, all the time avoiding public worship until, whilst at Thirsk, they boarded with a Wesleyan family. On a Sunday evening late in 1772 the young men accompanied the family to service, and Brunskill was greatly moved by the preaching. For some time he oscillated between anguish of soul and assurance, and during this period (1773) he married Sarah Hewitson, a dissenter of Ravenstonedale. They returned to the Orton district and shortly settled on a small farm there. Brunskill found solace in a book entitled *Principles of Methodism,* from which he learned that 'God wrought differently on different persons, – some having a full assurance of God's favour at first, whilst in others the work is more gradual'.[69]

At last, under his father's guidance, a small Methodist society was established at Orton, and Stephen was greatly helped by Mr. Story, the circuit minister, at whose intiative the young man joined the class meeting. Temptations to atheism, deism, and to the belief that 'the Alcoran might be as true as the Bible' followed,[70] but at last Brunskill came to the truth. He had next to stand the test of the ardent Calvinism of his father in law, and of the latter's minister at Ravenstonedale – an uncompromising exponent of double predestination, and an ardent foe of Rome. It was only after much prayer, we learn, that Stephen was able to save his own wife from the Calvinistic 'delusion'.[71]

In 1774 Brunskill was appointed class leader, and on Christmas Day of the same year he delivered his first word of exhortation.[72] He accepted preaching invitations from several places around, and the work grew. By 1784, the year in which his father died, the number of Wesleyans in Orton had increased to such an extent that it was necessary to hire a room to accommodate them.[73] In 1786 a severe 'nervous fever' smote Brunskill, and Mr. Thomas Shaw of Ravenstonedale, who afterwards became a travelling preacher, was a tower of strength to the family in their hour of need.

After his recovery, in 1787, Stephen felt moved to preach in Kendal,[74] not least because there was not another local preacher within twenty miles of that town. With a fellow preacher from Gamblesby and three friends from Alston Moor he journeyed to the town. His application to the proprietor for permission to preach in the old playhouse in the Market Place was granted, but in the event he addressed a large crowd from its steps. Curwen relates that on one occasion Brunskill had been warning his hearers that 'if they did not mend their ways, they would rush to hell in waggon loads'. Whereupon an old waggoner, Bet Craiston, cried, 'Whya, whya, Stephen, that's o'reet enough, but wha's to bring t'innocent horses back, I wonder? Tell me that, if thoo can.'[75]

On the approach of winter Brunskill informed his congregation that no more meetings could be held out of doors. This prompted a Mr. and Mrs. Barlow, late of Manchester, to offer two towards the six guineas needed to rent the old playhouse for a year. The remaining four guineas was collected, and the playhouse was taken. Soon, and despite the opposition of some local Christians, a society was formed and, acting on Brunskill's information, travelling preachers from the Barnard Castle circuit began fortnightly preaching visits to Kendal. On 13th February 1795 the playhouse was sold to the Wesleyans for £89. Soon they moved to 'The Fold', Stricklandgate, and there they remained until, on 30th October 1808 they opened a new chapel with accommodation for seven hundred people.

Stephen Brunskill, meanwhile, had taken a farm at Helsington in February 1790, and there he formed a Wesleyan society. After further removals to Witherslack and Milnthorpe, he was able to buy his own farm back at Orton. Later he bought a large house at the centre of the village. The house had been occupied by Independents who had hoped to establish a cause at Orton. Instead, Brunskill used the place as a Wesleyan meeting house, and secured the services of travelling preachers from the Brough circuit.[76] In 1811 he claimed a membership of between 30 and 40, local Independent competition notwithstanding.[77] Mrs. Brunskill died on 25th March 1823, but this in no way affected Stephen's zeal. He wrote pamphlets in which he defended Methodism (1798), advocated the doctrine of Christian perfection, and discussed the doctrine of the eternal Sonship of Christ; and he published a two-part work entitled *Dialogue between a Minister and one of his parishioners and others* in which he sought to 'expose the danger of having the form of godliness without the power'.[78] On 5th January 1827 he wrote that even after fifty-two years of preaching he could deliver three sermons on a Sunday with tolerable ease.[79] He lived to see the Orton

Wesleyan chapel opened in 1833 – indeed, he travelled as far as Kendal to raise subscriptions for it, and in return his fellow members honoured him by inviting him to preach the opening sermon.[80] His earnest desire that he might preach on Christmas Day 1835, the sixtieth anniversary of his first sermon, was granted, and on 2nd July 1836 he died aged 87 years.

We have accorded considerable space to Stephen Brunskill, not only because the details of his interesting life are not widely available, but more because he illustrates the great part played by local people in the establishment of Westmorland nonconformity. Like Fox before them, the great men of the Revival needed ardent local support if their proclamation was to bear churchly fruit.

Stephen Brunskill has one further service to render us. At one point in particular his *Life* illuminates a hitherto obscure corner of Kendal's nonconformist history, as we shall proceed to show. In the course of his account of the Lowther Street Congregational cause Nightingale writes, 'In the list of students educated at Lady Huntingdon's College, Trevecca, appears a Mr. Gray, who is given as settling at Kendal, but of him I have no information'.[81] He further supplies a footnote: 'The Rev. Daniel Gray, from this college, was for many years minister at Bootle, in Cumberland, but whether he had previously settled at Kendal is not known'.[82] The ambiguity of certain portions of the available evidence notwithstanding, we wish to suggest that Daniel Gray did minister at Kendal, though to a congregation of the Countess of Huntingdon's Connexion, and not at Lowther Street.

The ordination of Daniel Gray at Kendal in April 1782 is noted in *Life and Times.*[83] (The same volume elsewhere records the ordination of a Daniel Gray in London on 16th July 1783).[84] A letter dated 21st February 1782 from Lady Huntingdon to Gray refers to the possibility of a call's being addressed to him by the Kendal congregation. However, 'I by no means approve your accepting or hearing of anything till I see you'.[85] This letter further implies that Gray was at Bootle at the time of writing, and that the Countess had Wiltshire in mind as his future sphere of service. On 12th April 1782 the Countess wrote to the trustees of the Kendal meeting, who had by now called Gray to be their minister. She points out that Gray has yet to complete his training at Trevecca, and reminds them that she favours a connexional rather than an independent pattern of ministry. However, if the Kendal members approve her terms, 'and any proposals come, occasioning no division in the congregation of Kendal . . . you may depend upon a final answer from me, united with Mr. Gray's resolutions.'[86]

It appears from Lady Huntingdon's letter to Gray that she envisages separation from both Anglicans and dissenters: 'The objections to the Dissenters' plan [i.e. of ministry] are many, and the Church even more; that secession means the neutrality between both, and so materially offensive to neither'.[87] Two letters from Gray to the Countess reinforce the suggestion that a separate congregation of the Connexion is envisaged. On 4th December 1783 he wrote:

> 'Some time ago I sent your Ladyship a letter respecting affairs at Kendal, but have been rather surprised that no answer came. We are distressed respecting raising the purchase Money for the Meeting which is 150£. and it must be paid next Candlemass the 13th of February. We could borrow the 100£. but no one will advance the whole sum so that if your Ladyship would advance the odd fifty pounds as your Ladyship promised to assist it would make things quite happy . . . The Meeting is crowded exceedingly every Sabbath, and the Word appears to be blessed to many precious souls. It would grieve me to the heart if it should not go forward. Our Congregation at present is the largest and most flourishing one in the Town of Kendal, and if it is not properly settled by Candlemass, and the work should decrease, it would make the Dissenters triumph who have ever been bitter and persecuting both you and me and the connection in general . . .'[88]

Gray further mentions that the people have suggested that he put his own money into the cause, but he considers that such an action would tie him too closely to the one place, and deprive him of that measure of ministerial mobility which he desires.

Since we have no evidence that Lowther Street was financially embarrassed (but rather the reverse in view of funds received from the Scotch chapel), we incline to query the identification of Gray with Lowther Street. Our hesitation is confirmed by a letter of 3rd February 1794 from Gray to Lady Huntingdon. He here commends a young man (unnamed) for training at Trevecca: 'I think he will be an honer to the Connection'. He continues: 'he attends the Worship of God at the New Meeting where I was chosen in but afterwards refused but he is not joined in society with them. They have persuaded him to go to the dissenting Academy in Yorkshire but he has been with me, and would rather enter into our Connection . . . I send you this letter by his Desire to know whether you are willing he should go to the College . . .'[89] The implication here is that the Connexion's cause differs from that at the New Chapel (i.e. Lowther Street). Moreover, the Gray-Huntingdon correspondence more than spans the known ministry of James Kenworthy at Lowther Street. Kenworthy was ordained at Kendal in 1783, and had removed to Warrington before 1794. A third letter to the Countess, written on 2nd April 1788 and signed by W. George, Flavell Irving, Thomas Mackreth and George Woof, makes it plain that not all the money required for the purchase of the meeting place is yet to hand. Moreover, 'there are some of the troublers of Israel that has crept amongst us into Kendal that draws the simple and the unstable from the truth as it is in Jesus to embrace Mr. Wesley's gospel instead of the Lord our Righteousness . . . I would to God they were cut off . . .'[90] All of which brings us full circle to Stephen Brunskill.

We have referred to opposition from Christians encountered by Brunskill in Kendal in 1787. In fact he is quite definite as to his opponents: they were of the Countess of Huntingdon's Connexion. The Connexion's preachers were in the habit of using the old playhouse,[91] and some eight members of their congregation attended Brunskill's preaching for a short while.[92] At this

> 'The minister began to be afraid of losing his flock. He therefore called them together and represented us in an unfavourable light as being self-righteous and holding the doctrines of the Church of Rome, etc. He did all in his

power to prevent our prosperity; and as the Methodists and their principles were but little known in Kendal, too much credit was given to his false and slanderous accusations.'[93]

As noted earlier, on 13th February 1795 Brunskill and his followers purchased the old playhouse in which the Countess of Huntingdon's congregation had met, and this year coincides with that given in our sources for the departure from Kendal of Daniel Gray. We conclude that Gray ministered to the Countess of Huntingdon's Kendal congregation, and not to that at Lowther Street. There is no evidence to suggest that the Calvinistic Methodists who subsequently met in the Kirkland conventicle under the leadership of George Robinson incorporated the remnant of the Connexion's congregation, though they may have done.[94] Certainly there is no reference to the Connexion in the 1836 government list of *Dissenting Meeting Houses.*

In the year of Benjamin Ingham's death, 1772, the Westmorland Quakers were visited by *their* celebrated itinerant, John Woolman, as the following extract from his *Journal* shows:

'23 day 8 mo. Was this day at Preston Patrick . . . and had a comfortable meeting.
26 day 8 mo. Being now at George Crosfield's in Westmorland . . . I rested a few days in body and mind with our Friend Jane Crosfield who was once in America. Was on Sixth day of the week at Kendal in Westmorland and at Grayrigg meeting the 30 day 8 mo. and first of the week.'[95]

We are also informed that he is now reducing the number of meetings he attends.[96] On 22nd September John Woolman, now in York, addressed a letter to John Wilson, his Kendal host, in which he said, "When I was at your home, I believe I had a sense of the pride of people being gratified in some of the business thou followest, and I feel a concern in pure love to endeavour to inform thee of it".[97] Wilson's business was that of shearman dyer, and the erstwhile tailor, John Woolman, had a marked preference for cleaned as against dyed garments. The following extract from a letter written after Woolman's death on 7th October by Sarah Hall to Deborah

Shackleton reveals more of Woolman's personal characteristics:

> 'He chose to walk. He was very particular in his dress. He wore a coarse cloth like flannel, no cuffs to his coat, a drab hat, a coarse unbleached shirt, no stock or neckcloth, white woolen stockings, shoes uncurried, the native colour, tied with the same. He drank no foreign liquors or tea. He did not choose to drink out of silver or make use of silver spoons. Herb tea sometimes he drank, sweetened with honey. Sugar he never chose. He was indeed a strking pattern of temperance and humility.'[98]

For all that, 'His deep concern for the welfare of others than Friends – slaves in America, sailors at sea, post boys and farm laborers and city dwellers in England – was not unusual among Friends, though seemingly inconsistent with their individual introspectiveness and their sectarian concentration'.[99] We may well believe that some of this concern rubbed off on the increasingly socially conscious Westmorland Friends.

The Friends' school at Stramongate continued throughout the eighteenth century. In 1715 John Jopson was succeeded as headmaster by Thomas Rebanks, whose period of service extended over half a century. In 1728 the school became a public boarding school, and it was to become increasingly undenominational in character. At the time of the Rebellion of 1745 Rebanks found himself the unwilling host to a party of Jacobites who descended on the school, and ransacked it as they left. George Bewley was headmaster from 1756, and by 1772 the success of the school, and the enthusiasm of such men as Isaac Wilson of Windermere, made possible the opening of new buildings on a portion of the Bryan Lancaster estate. When his assistant George Raw left in 1775, Bewley invited his cousin Jonathan Dalton to assist him. In 1781 Jonathan was joined by his fifteen-year-old brother John,[100] who was to spend twelve years in Kendal laying the foundation for that scientific career which was to win him world acclaim. Bewley retired in 1785 and his mantle fell upon Jonathan Dalton, who held undistinguished office for thirty years. Sadly, the boarders left with Bewley, and the reputation of the Daltons as schoolmasters was not high: 'They were uncompromising in their discipline, and somewhat over stern in punishment, although John was the milder of the two, and was, besides, too much absorbed in private study to look out for delinquencies'.[101]

Despite the influence of John Woolman, the developing social conscience, and the continuing work of the school; and notwithstanding the fact that in 1777 Nicolson and Burn had to admit that 'several of the considerable tradesmen' of Kendal were Quakers,[102] the overriding impression we have of Westmorland Quakers in the eighteenth century is one of increasing respectability at the expense of early zeal. Friends were now much more likely to be solid citizens than zealous catalysts. Perhaps the *closure* during the century of meetings at Poolbank, Langdale and Shap is a symptom of the fairly widespread malaise which had overtaken them.

Whereas the dissenting academies and the Quaker schools are products of seventeenth century concern, the distinctively new educational product of the eighteenth century – and of the Revival in particular – is the Sunday School. Dr. Paul Sangster considers that 'the most important educational development of the eighteenth century is the Sunday School.'[103] This movement for popular (and, originally, secular) education had reached Kendal by 1785. By 1787 there were schools at Cordwainer's Hall; Redman's Yard No. 1; Redman's Yard No. 2; The Hospital; Fox's Yard; and Royal Oak.[104] The schools catered for 270 pupils, and subscriptions amounted to £68/4/0½. Of this £31/12/0 was expended on masters' salaries. The responsible committee was broadly based, and it is noteworthy that the schools were by no means the exclusive preserve of trinitarian evangelicals. On the contrary, in Kendal Caleb Rotheram the younger actively supported the movement, and in 1799 the local committee's secretary was Henry Robinson, Vicar of Kendal – a man of presumed unitarian views.[105] We learn that by the turn of the century

> 'Rooms were rented in various parts of the town, to the number, at one time, of eight or more, and in these rooms, reading and writing were taught. The masters received 2s. each Sunday, and 6d extra when there was a fire. The

> superintendents were appointed monthly from amongst the subscribers. Each scholar had to learn the Catechism, and to attend divine service in the Parish Church in the morning and afternoon, unless the parents of any child desiring it to accompany them to their own place of worship, chose to call for it instead. At one time as many as 800 children were in attendance at these schools. The masters kept the roll, and every boy who attended regularly both morning and afternoon for the 52 Sundays of the year, received a grey swallow-tail coat. This coat, however, became in time so peculiar that it was judiciously changed in after years for a fustian jacket. The girls *probably* received grey frocks on the same terms.'[106]

The first denominational Sunday School appears to have been that at Lowther Street, founded in 1789; and in 1793 the energetic James Hill of Ravenstonedale founded the earliest rural Sunday School to have come to our notice.

IV – THE NINETEENTH CENTURY

By the time of Stephen Brunskill's death in 1836, Wesleyan Methodism was firmly rooted in many parts of the county. A Sunday School was commenced at Kendal in 1814, and on Thursday 29th March 1883 the chapel, now enlarged and renovated, was opened, and the occasion was marked by the visit of the President of the Conference, the Revd. Charles Garrett, and one of his predecessors in office, the Revd. W. B. Pope, D.D.[1] Meanwhile interesting developments had been taking place at circuit level. The Kendal circuit returned 775 members in 1850. 'The Lord's Day Plan of the Wesleyan Methodist Preachers in the Kendal Circuit, 1848–9'[2] serves a circuit of 28 stations stretching from Wray, Lancashire, to Ambleside, and from Bowness to Gayle near Hawes, Yorkshire. There are four ministers, Messrs. Lewis, Baylis, Dunbar and Huddleston, all of whom live in Kendal; 39 preachers on full plan; 4 probationers; and 6 exhorters. Proceeds from the sale of plans at 2d each are to be devoded to the Local Preachers' Horse Hire Fund. The Westmorland stations on this plan are: Kendal Kirkland, Kirkby Lonsdale, Staveley, Beathwaite Green, Milnthorpe, Ambleside, Ravenstonedale, Burnside, Gatebeck, Whinfell, Mealbank, Hutton, Hutton Roof, Lupton, Crook, and Bowness and Troutbeck. Of these Lupton, Hutton and Milnthorpe do not appear on an 1854 plan.

In 1854 the Hawes circuit was carved out of the unwieldy Kendal circuit, and Benjamin N. Haworth became the first minister. 1871 saw a further division when the new Sedbergh circuit was formed from Hawes. Among the Sedbergh societies was one in Westmorland. The Kendal plan for 1853–4 shows that Ellerhill, Merthwaite and Sandbed farms are subsumed under 'Ravenstonedale'. On 27th October 1861 a chapel for the area was opened at a cost of £208. Until 1870 it was known as Ravenstonedale, and thereafter as Fell End. Membership fluctuated: 18 in 1854, 51 in 1859, 39 when the chapel was opened, and 26 one year later. In 1882 the Sedbergh circuit returned 279 members, but by 1900 membership had declined to 165, and the circuit was joined to that of Kirkby Stephen and Appleby. This arrangement, which resulted in a vast circuit, was never entirely approved of by the Sedbergh members, and in 1919 Sedbergh became independent once more, and continues so to this day.[3]

Fell End (Wesleyan) Methodist chapel.

As for the north of the county, in 1803 Brough (which returned 178 members in 1804) was disjoined from the Barnard Castle circuit, and became a circuit in its own right. In 1818 Brough and Penrith were linked, with a total membership of 465. This arrangement lasted until 1825, when the areas were separated once more, and from 1825–77 Appleby was the head of the circuit. 327 members were recorded in 1826, and 576 in 1850, and this despite the fact that by the latter date Baptists, and Primitive and Free Methodists were active in the area. Mr. J. Walker Nicholson had access to some Wesleyan preaching plans of the Brough and Penrith circuit dating back to 1820. These showed that regular Sunday services were held at Appleby, Brough, Brough Sowerby, Bolton, Cliburn, Clifton, Crosby Garrett, Crackenthorpe,

The roofless shell of the old Wesleyan chapel, Appleby.

Dufton, Kirkby Stephen, Kirkby Thore, Long Marton, Morland, Murton, Oxenthwaite (Stainmore), Temple Sowerby and Warcop. Soulby appeared for the first time in 1824. The Kirkoswald circuit, with Temple Sowerby among its societies, was formed out of the Penrith circuit in 1871. Penrith, apart from its period of association with Brough (1818–25), had been an independent circuit since 1806, and continues so to this day.

Appleby (Wesleyan) Methodist chapel.

The Westmorland Lake District was the last area of the county to yield to Wesleyanism, and Ambleside was the scene of its first success. As we shall shortly see, the Revd. J. A. Coombs established an Independent cause in the town. In 1842 Mrs. Parks, a Wesleyan, came to Ambleside in service, attended the Independent chapel, and there met a fellow Methodist, Mary Brown of Penrith. Shortly other Methodists, including William Creighton, came to the town, and they were in a position to purchase the Independent chapel on Mr. Coomb's departure from the district. The Ambleside society was joined to Kendal circuit, and the work soon spread. The following extracts from reports will provide some indication both of the progress made, and of the opposition sustained:

> 28th December 1866: 'Four cottage services are maintained . . . At Bowness several persons have recently joined our church. At Windermere our congregations and Sunday-school have increased in numbers . . . Everywhere strong Episcopal prejudices exist . . . At Grasmere much prejudice is arrayed against us. We have been refused two eligible rooms, but have secured and fitted up a place for our services.[4]
>
> 3rd January 1870: 'Many striking cases of conversion have occurred. I am encouraged by the spiritual prosperity, by the efficient working of our members, and by their hearty co-operation in the prosecution of our Mission.'[5]
>
> 29th June 1872: 'We make progress, notwithstanding "low" Church influence and "high" Church prejudice. Efforts are not wanting to induce parents to take their children from our Sunday-schools and to send them to "Church" schools.'[6]
>
> 1st March 1873: 'Very active clerical opposition here seeks to injure our Sunday-schools, and to hinder and destroy our work. We are not damaged by this impotent exhibition of bigotry . . . many lost ones have been brought to God.'[7]

Despite such opposition, the work progressed. At Grasmere a Mr. Robert Hayton collected more than £63 towards a new chapel building, and this was supplemented by a donation of £50 from Mr. W. T. Whelpton of London, who had, in addition, bought the site for £42/12/0. The foundation stone was laid in June 1873, the total cost of the building was £700, and on 4th June 1874 Joshua Mason, the Chairman of the Carlisle District, conducted the opening service. In 1878 Ambleside became head of a circuit. But in 1900, now week-end, it was reunited with Kendal. Today it stands independent once more, and thanks to the increasing accessibility and desirability of the Lake District, its membership has trebled during this century. By contrast, the membership of the Kendal circuit has increased by about one eighth, and that of the Kirkby Stephen and Appleby circuit has declined by approximately one third.

We should not be misled into thinking that Anglican opposition was the only obstacle to Wesleyan progress. Sometimes the zeal of the faithful flagged. Hence, for example, the *Pastoral Address to the Wesleyan Methodist Societies in the Appleby Circuit, by the Ministers,* 1855.[8] The ministers pull no punches. 'The Circuit is an assemblage of small places, no one of which is able to exercise a satisfactory influence over the rest, by taking the lead: – in fact, it is a *Circuit without a head* . . . System is lamentably wanting; and Methodist discipline needs carrying out in all its parts with vigour and efficiency.' Chapels are poorly kept; the legal status of some of them has not been properly secured; the people are not giving as they might. Nevertheless, 'the GREAT HEAD of the Church is waiting to pour out a rich and abundant blessing, the instant that Methodism, by becoming truly and fully awake to its duty, becomes prepared to receive it'. Nine years later conditions were little better:

> 'The want of ministerial labour and pastoral care is painfully felt in this [i.e. the Appleby] Circuit. There are twenty-five preaching places on the plan, and these extend over twenty-eight miles. Our labours are dissipated into inefficiency, and no one place can have that attention which is necessary to prosperity.'[9]

Difficulties notwithstanding, Wesleyanism spread, and by the turn of the century its chapels covered the county, and before the century was into its third decade some of them were celebrating their centenaries.[10] Like the other groups of Methodists to whom we shall shortly turn, the Wesleyans owed much to their local preachers, many of them rough-hewn, who undertook arduous journeys in all weathers for the Gospel's sake. No doubt when the bicycle was included under the Horse Hire Fund of the Kirkby Stephen and Appleby circuit in 1909 the preachers rejoiced. A preacher was permitted to hire a bicycle in order to reach his appointment, provided that the chapel to be visited was more than five miles distant, and that there was no other means of reaching it. It is further refreshing to record, as an antidote to the sometimes stuffy impression conveyed by Wesleyan ministers of the Bunting type, that some of the Wesleyan ministers in Westmorland were more than a little eccentric. Prominent in this regard was the Revd. Hodgson Casson of the Brough circuit (1819/20). Through his wife he owned some property, and this permitted him to vote in the General Election of 1820. At Appleby polling booth he thundered that he would refuse to vote unless his occupation were recorded as 'fisher of men'.

The present-day Baptist presence in Westmorland owes its existence on the one hand to the determination and enthusiasm of north-eastern Baptists,[11] and on the other hand to the increase of Baptist influence at Crosby Garrett following the arrival there of Mr. and Mrs. George Greenwood. The first north-eastern initiative, however, proved to be short-lived. In 1799 the Revd. Charles Whitfield[12] of Hamsterley bought the old Independent Chapel at Kirkby Stephen from Isabella Hutchinson for £86. (She had purchased it from Mr. Robinson of Crosby Garrett for £60 in 1786). A Baptist meeting was established at Brough in 1806, but no records survive. Presumably, however, Mary Robson was a member there, for it was she who bought the Kirkby Stephen chapel from Mr. Whitfield in 1812. The cause did not thrive, and in 1814 the building was again sold, this time to Edward Richardson, an Independent. Apart from the Unitarian Baptist movement in Kendal we hear no more of Baptists in Westmorland until 1827.

In 1810 James Kay,[13] who had been ordained to Lowther Street Independent church on 29th July 1801, left the pastorate on account of his having embraced unitarian and baptist beliefs. For a time he led a congregation of Unitarian Baptists who met in the Caledonian Room, Market Place, and performed baptism in the river Kent and in the Anchorites' Well.[14] Kay left Kendal in 1817 and began to preach for the Methodist Unitarians (presumably in Lancashire). There followed a brief pastorate at the old Presbyterian (now Unitarian) church Hindley (1819–21). In 1821 Kay departed for America, where he ministered to unitarians at Northumberland, Pennsylvania from 1821–46. A short time after he left them his Kendal congregation dwindled to such a low number that most of the surviving members joined the Market Place Unitarian church, and the Unitarian Baptist cause ceased.

The Inghamites meanwhile were in decline. With reference to the disunity which followed Allen's embracing of Sandemanianism, and his break with Ingham, William Romaine wrote c.1780: 'There was a blessed work of God among the people, till that horrid blast from the North came and destroyed all'.[15] It is said that whereas prior to 1759 there were between 80 and 90 Inghamite chapels, that number was swiftly and drastically reduced to about 13.[16] Of these the cause at Kendal was one. John Huck held the office of elder there from 1804 until his death in 1845. For part of this time (1807–26) John Pearson rendered great service, not least as a preacher, though he never held the office of elder. In 1826 he emigrated to America. Burials took place in the chapel yard at Kendal from 1756 (Elizabeth Pratt) to 1855 (Archibald Watt).

The remaining Inghamites had by now become associated with kindred souls in Scotland. In 1814, through the efforts of John Pearson a union was achieved with the Daleites or Old Scots Independents. The founders of this latter group had been influenced ecclesiologically by John Glas, for all that they denied that they were Glasites.[17]

The government Register for 1836 shows that both the Glasites and the Inghamites (branded 'Jughamites' by a delightful misprint!) had places of worship in Kendal. The Glasites' meeting house was built in 1824 in Windmill, or Post Office Yard. Benjamin Pearson was the presiding elder. Soon the cause declined, and some members joined the Inghamites. Curwen thinks that c.1846 the property was sold to the Revd. Robert Braithwaite.[18] By the time of the 1851 census there were but 9 Inghamite chapels and 6 Sandemanian chapels in the whole of England. By the time Tyerman wrote in 1873 he could report that 6 Inghamite chapels only remained: at Winewall, Wheatley, Todmorden, Tadcaster, Leeds and Kendal.[19] The life of the Kendal Inghamite cause came to an end c.1970.

The nineteenth century developments of Congregationalism[20] in Westmorland can only be described as sporadic and, in many cases, transient. Unlike some other counties, Westmorland did not benefit from county-wide, systematic home missionary endeavour. This is not to say that there was *no* interest in the county from beyond its boundaries: there was, and in time Westmorland's Congregational churches came to be shared between the Lancashire and Yorkshire Congregational Unions. It is, however, a local initiative, undertaken as the new century approached, which comes first to our attention:

> 'A successful attempt has been made to spread the Gospel in the neighbouring towns and villages of Ravenstonedale. The Ministers have preached at Kirbysteven, Rookby, Caber and Crosly [i.e. Kirkby Stephen, Rookby, Kaber and Crosby Garrett]; and so great is the number of hearers, that they have been obliged frequently to preach out of doors. The utmost attention is paid to the word, and many are enquiring the way to Zion with their face thitherward.'[21]

No doubt the leadership of James Hill was operative here.

Hill's successor, James Muscutt, who was ordained at Ravenstonedale on 12th June 1811, accepted the charge 'on condition that the Church be reorganised and put upon the Independent or Congregational plan'. Apparently authority in the church was in the hands of a few members only, and Muscutt disapproved of this.[22] Muscutt, who removed to Cockermouth in 1815, was followed by Robert Hamilton Bonner (1817–35), and he by William Hassell. Hassell was inducted in 1836, but in 1838 he seceded to the Wesleyans. The Ravenstonedale Wesleyan chapel was built for him and his sympathisers in 1839. As far as we know this is the only case of the formation of a Westmorland Methodist cause as a consequence of secession from a church of Old Dissent. Nightingale and Whitehead quote *The Kendal Mercury* report of 1836 which speaks of the dilapidated state of Ravenstonedale's Independent chapel and grounds, and continues, 'We are told also that no more than half a dozen persons now go to worship there'. A new deed dated 26th May 1836, and the reconstitution of the church (now comprising 7 women and 3 men) on 5th August 1838, paved the way for a fresh start. Among the later ministers were Walter Mathieson (1847–56), who also served the Independents at Crosby Garrett; and William Nicholls (1869–83),[23] the historian of the district. Towards the end of the century the evening congregation numbered about 100.

Farther north, local initiatives were again taken, as the following report of 1811 makes plain:

> 'Some Independent Ministers, of the counties of Westmorland and Cumberland, having formed an Association for the spread of Gospel in those benighted parts of the nation, – a Meeting was held at Alston, Cumberland, April 17, when two sermons were preached by Mr. Scott, of Hexham, and Mr. Muscutt, of Ravenstonedale. It was resolved that a Student be procured immediately from Hackney, to labour as an Itinerant in the town and vicinity of Appleby, Westmorland. The Ministers of this Association have preached in Appleby, and in nine or ten villages adjacent, and formed a church of about 16 members. The congregation are in general numerous and attentive, but very barely supplied with gospel preaching. We have been able to obtain as much pecuniary assistance as will support an Itinerant; and hope contributions will increase . . . Mr. Dickenson of Dufton, Treasurer; and Mr. Norris, Alston, Secretary.'[24]

The following year the Association reported that their 'itinerancy in the neighbourhood of Appleby, is flourishing'.[25] A similar statement was made by the Associated Ministers (now under their new name, 'The Northern Congregational Association') in 1813, though they added that 'pecuniary resources are very inadequate . . . '[26] The 1814 Report declared that in view of the success of the itinerancy additional plans for evangelism were being made;[27] there was a further glowing report for 1815[28] – and there regular reports to the journals appear to end. By 1827 William Selby was minister at Appleby, and he also had oversight of the church at Temple Sowerby, in which village a building had been converted into a chapel in 1813.[29] The Temple Sowerby church appeared for the last time in *CYB* in 1856, and we may suppose that the other causes in the district ceased before this time. Certainly, by the time Nightingale wrote *LN* he could say that they became extinct many years ago.[30]

In 1814 the Independents of Kirkby Stephen, as earlier mentioned, bought a chapel in New Inn Yard, which had previously been used by Sandemanians and Baptists. John Capper was ordained there on 8th April 1824.[31] For a time in the mid 1840's the Kirkby Stephen and Ravenstonedale Independents co-operated as a united church. Again, from 1857–63 the two churches formed a joint pastorate. On May 17th 1864 J. Jackson laid the foundation stone of a new chapel at Kirkby Stephen,[32] and in the following year the building was opened at a cost of £1,150. An associated chapel at Nateby, built in 1873, was subsequently handed over to the Wesleyans, before being sold in 1913 for £200. Braithwaite mentions an Independent mission room at Hartley. The Kirkby Stephen church, whose membership exceeded 100 c.1884, made its last appearance in *CYB* in 1945.

Kirkby Stephen Congregational chapel (now R.C.).

Coming south we find that on 26th November 1815 the Revd. Joseph France of High Street Congregational church, Lancaster, preached at Kirkby Lonsdale with the blessing of the Lancashire Union.[33] The West Riding Itinerant Society in the person of its founder's son, the Revd. John Cockin[34] of Holmfirth, supported the venture, as did the Revd. Robert Maclean[35] of Kendal. At first a rented room was used, and then:

> 'Oct. 2 [1816] a neat Chapel was opened at Kirkby Lonsdale, Westmoreland. The Rev. J. France, A.M. of Lancaster preached in the morning . . . Mr. Maclean of Kendal, in the afternoon . . . and Mr. Eccles of Leeds, in the evening . . . This beautifully situated town has long been viewed with feelings of commiseration by the friends of the gospel . . . now the most pleasing hopes are indulged of permanent success.'[36]

The chapel cost £400, and in 1817 William Maclean (presumed to be the son of Robert) came to be minister. He and his successors also conducted occasional services in such surrounding villages and hamlets at Hutton Roof, Barbon, Whittington, Kearstwick, Ireby and Old Town. The ardently sought 'permanent success' was elusive. In 1830 the church was dissolved and then re-organised; at times it was worked with Wray, Lancashire, and then with Milnthorpe, the scene of discontinuous dissenting activity since the seventeenth century. (As early as 31st August 1691 the Presbyterian Fund had voted £8 p.a. to provide a monthly lecture at Milnthorpe. The first such lecture was given by Thomas Jollie on 29th September). At Wray the Revd. S. Bell of Lancaster officiated at the opening in March 1833 of a place of worship provided by the sister of the Anglican incumbent of Bentham, but such generosity did not prevent the Kirkby Lonsdale Congregationalists from opening a day school at their chapel in 1850 'to counteract the strong and baneful influence of High Churchism in the town'. A report of three years later tells a sorry tale of the church's being 'torn by internal dissention [and] all but abandoned for the present'. From 1855 it revived. The chapel was rebuilt on the same site and re-opened on 13th May 1888, during the fruitful ministry of the

Revd. Matthew Henry Sharp, who remained at his post from November 1861 to 19th October 1890.[37] The cause at Kirkby Lonsdale was last noted in *CYB* in 1964.

The Milnthorpe church had an even shorter life. In September 1818 a room was opened there for worship, and on 5th March 1820 a converted building was opened as a chapel, Mr. Stowell, a student at Blackburn academy, and Mr. Greatbach of North Meols preaching the sermons. The report of the proceedings expressed the hope 'that this will soon be an important Itinerant station, under the fostering care of the Lancashire County Union, and the kind friends at Kendal. The Chapel has been built at the sole expense of a gentleman at the latter place [i.e. Henry Hewitson]'.[38] The Revd. Jospeh Smedley became pastor in 1820, and in 1821 it was reported that Milnthorpe had a congregation of 200. In the same year a church of 14 members was formed. Smedley left in April 1822, and during the summer of 1823 James Hargraves came to Milnthorpe from Idle academy. He was ordained and inducted to the pastorate on 29th July 1824,[39] and the church was reconstituted. Nearby at Burton in Kendal, where services had been held since 1818, there was a congregation of nearly 100. The success in the area was not maintained, however, The work at Burton declined, and the opening in 1837 of a new Anglican church at Milnthorpe greatly affected the Congregational cause there. The chapel was shortly closed, only to be reopened in 1839. Once again the church, now with 10 members, was reconstituted in 1843,[40] but further decline ensued. After a chequered history of brief pastorates and local difficulties the members disbanded, and the building was finally sold in 1866.

Among other churches in the county which enjoyed but a brief existence was that at Orton. We learn from Stephen Brunskill's *Life*[41] that the Independents were very active in Orton whilst he was attempting to establish Wesleyanism there. Again, on 7th April 1824 an Independent chapel built at the expense of Mr. Charles Davies, was opened at Brough.[42] John Capper of Kirkby Stephen supplied it in 1826, and it was later converted into dwelling houses. Capper also supplied the chapel at Birks which had previously been occupied by Inghamites and Baptists, and which came into Independent hands in 1829. Of this chapel Whellan writes, 'it is now [1860] used for farming purposes, and occasionally for preaching'.[43]

It appears that the hey-day of Congregationalist expansion in Westmorland in the first half of the nineteenth century was c.1829. In that year the following details were published:[44]

Place	Pastor	Remarks
Appleby	Revd. Wm. Selby	
Brough	Revd. J. Capper	
Burton		Supplied by neighbouring ministers.
Holme	Revd. G. Hoyle	
Kendal	Revd. D. Jones	
Kirkby Lonsdale	Revd. S. Healey	
Kirkby Stephen	Revd. J. Capper	Mr. C. visits eight stations
Milnthorpe	Revd. G. Hoyle	
Ravenstonedale	Revd. J. Bonner	
Stainton	Revd. D. Jones	
Sedgwick	Revd. G. Hoyle	
Temple Sowerby	Revd. – (*sic*) Selby	Home Missionary Station

Despite all the effort, Slate could inform his readers in 1840 that in Westmorland 'there is but *one* Congregational church able to maintain its own pastor, whilst there is an immense tract of country, with numerous villages, whose inhabitants are awfully ignorant of the only way of salvation'.[45]

The Lake District yielded last to the Congregationalists as to the other nineteenth century evangelicals. The Revd. J. A. Coombs,[46] who had recently moved to Belle Vue, Ambleside, after a lengthy ministry in Salford, opened a room in his house for worship in the spring of 1839. In November 1840 a church was formed, whose membership soon reached 30. Growth continued, and soon Thomas Wilson bought and presented a plot of land on which a chapel was erected, and opened in October 1841.[47] Shortly after Coombs's departure from the district in 1847 the chapel was sold to the Wesleyans. In 1857 the Troutbeck Bridge church was opened at a cost of £500; and in 1880 the Carver Memorial Church, Windermere, was built by the family of William Carver of Manchester as a memorial to himself. Troutbeck Bridge made its last appearance in the final edition of *CYB*, 1972, but Carver continues to this day. The most recently erected Congregational chapel in Westmorland, that at Little Asby, was opened in September 1889. It does not appear in *CYB* after 1962.

Carver Memorial Congregational (now U.R.C.) church, Windermere.

We now turn to one of the most significant of the new departures of the nineteenth century, Primitive Methodism. Led by Hugh Bourne and William Clowes, the Primitive Methodist movement began early in the nineteenth century in the Mow Cop district of Staffordshire.[48] Unlike their New Connexion counterparts, the Primitive Methodists had no ecclesiological quarrel with Wesleyanism. Perhaps the strongest *non*-Wesleyan influence upon *some* of them, not least Hugh Bourne himself, was that of the Quakers.[49] They were at one in feeling that the early fire of revival had died down, and their objective was not schism, but the revitalising of the Wesleyan societies. Their methods – not least their predilection for aggressive evangelism and their camp meetings –

earned them the disapproval of many Wesleyan leaders. Eventually it was the expulsion of the Primitive Methodist leaders from the Wesleyan fold, despite Clowes's sincere attempts at pacification, which prompted the birth of the new denomination. Bourne was expelled by the Wesleyans in 1810, and in May of the following year jointly issued communion cards proclaimed the union of the Camp Meeting Methodists and the Clowesites. In February 1812 the name 'Primitive Methodist' was formally adopted.

The new movement spread northwards into Cheshire, eastwards into Nottinghamshire, and thence to Hull. Patterson described Hull as the 'Thessalonica of Primitive Methodism,' and certainly a vast army of missionary helpers was sent out from that town. The Hull mission soon spawned centres at Darlington and Barnard Castle, and when William Clowes visited the latter town on 22nd February 1822 he found a society of no fewer than 120 members. When the Sunderland district was formed in 1824 its sphere extended from the east coast to Hexham and Carlisle. We shall have to return to the Barnard Castle circuit shortly, but it was an independent mission under Hull's auspices which first reached Westmorland.

In May 1822 the Hull mission despatched Francis N. Jersey,[50] a former sailor, from Silsden near Bradford where he had been evangelising, to Kendal and district. At Kendal Jersey found quick success, a society was formed, and as early as 19th October 1823 William Clowes was able to preach at the opening of a new chapel there.[51] In the same year Kendal returned 189 members. Sadly the cause declined almost as quickly as it had grown, and this, together with the fact that its retention would have placed a considerable strain upon the denomination's financial resources, resulted in its temporary abandonment. However, in 1829 the Revd. Richard Cordingley of the Preston circuit revived the Kendal cause, and after a period as a mission of the Barnard Castle circuit, Kendal became an independent circuit in 1857. The Kendal members worshipped in a room above some cottages until their new chapel in Black Hall Yard, Stricklandgate, was opened by the Mayor, J. J. Wilson on 14th July 1870.[52] A Sunday School was commenced in 1823 by James and Robert Nelson and George Gaskell, and by 1880 it included 45 young men and women of whom 40 were church members.[53] The circuit remained within the Sunderland district until 1885, in which year it joined the Carlisle and Whitehaven district. By 1900 a further reorganisation had placed it within the Darlington and Stockton district. In 1900 Primitive Methodist chapels of the Kendal circuit were to be found at Stricklandgate, Staveley, Beckfoot, Fellside and Whinfell, and the total membership was 230.

Brough was the gateway to Westmorland for that evangelical thrust which the Primitive Methodists initiated from their base at Barnard Castle. Their pre-eminent missionary was Thomas Batty. Born in 1790, Batty served at sea until 1813. He then became a Wesleyan local preacher, but after he had preached at two camp meetings in the Driffield area he was required to choose between that kind of activity and Wesleyanism. He could not cease to evangelise by all possible means, and so in 1820 he turned to the Primitive Methodists. They sent him to the Silsden mission, and thence, in the autumn of 1822, to Barnard Castle. Almost exactly one year later he arrived in Brough. His fame had gone before him, and his successes already entitled him to be known as 'the apostle of Weardale'. A large audience heard his first address in Brough. Batty spoke from a horse block in front of an inn, and after the meeting a Brough Sowerby woman gave him hospitality. She was shortly converted, and soon a society was established in her house. Such were the prospects in the area that an additional missionary, Thomas Webb, was sent to assist Batty.

The gentry viewed Batty's arrival with dismay. They sought to intimidate him but undeterred, and in face of possible physical assault, Batty lauded that religious freedom which Englishmen enjoyed under the law! In the event he had no need to call upon the services of his bodyguard of Brough Sowerby and Kirkby Stephen men who were standing by. Batty's opponents next sent a crier through the town to announce a verstry meeting at which steps would be taken to put down all midnight revelling and ranting. Then one of Batty's friends engaged the crier to publish the fact that the laws against gaming, Sabbath-breaking and the like would be enforced, and that if the churchwardens and constables were dilatory in attending to such breaches as were detected they would be presented at the Bishop's court or quarter sessions. In Batty's own words:

> 'This intervention on the part of our friend, completely quashed the vestry meeting; it was never held while I remained in the country, – and after this publication we went on quietly, and had no more disturbance. A glorious work broke out immediately, and in a fortnight we added 30 souls to our society; and the work was both genuine and deep. Some of the most wicked characters, and others less so, were brought to the knowledge of the truth, 'and there was great joy in that town'. The old farmer who lent us his barn was also converted, and gave us a piece of land, on which a chapel was erected!'[54]

The indenture of 6th April 1825 between 'William Jackson of Church Brough, yeo., and Isabella his wife of the one part, and William Raine, grocer, and many others of the second part' makes quite plain the cause for which the land was sold:

> 'Whereas in 1810 was begun in England under the ministry of Hugh Bourne and James Bourne of Bemersley in the parish of Norton in the Moors, co. Stafford, a Society of Protestant Christians, now called Primitive Methodists, by some called "Ranters", and they having determined to build a Chapel or Meeting House at Church Brough, now for £6 the said Jackson and his wife sell to those of the second part a piece of ground . . .'[55]

The work progressed, and when in August 1831 Hugh Bourne himself visited Brough in order to attend the quarterly meeting of the Barnard Castle branch of the Hull circuit, he was able to record, 'In this branch there is a spirit of prayer and the work is in a good state'.[56]

The Brough Circuit Account Book records the following stations and memberships for the quarter ending 19th September 1845 (i.e. the oldest extant record): Brough 19; Blackmoregate 10; Mouthlock 20; Ormside 7; Espland Hill 7; Dufton 9; Schoolhouses 7; Sandford 10; Couplandbeck 0; Closehouses 9; Kaber 7; Hoff Row 3; Newbiggin 14; Teaby [*sic*] 0; Carlingill 6; Longdale 9; Roundthwaite 0; Flakebridge 0; Milburn 12; and Bleatarn 0 – a total of 140. Branch income for the quarter amounted to £11/17/3, of which

£2/1/7 was contributed by Mouthlock, where John Hilton the carrier rendered stalwart service. 'Schoolhouses' presumably refers to the meeting at North Stainmore which occupied a school house until the chapel was built in 1869. (It was superseded in 1910). Services at Blackmoregate were held in the home of William Alderson, and Kaber, where the first chapel was built in 1859 and its successor in 1891, was well blessed in Joseph Watson, who held office as circuit steward for twenty years.

There was an inevitable degree of fluidity in respect of these early meeting places. Some became established, others did not. Thus, when the Brough branch reported to the Sunderland District on 17th March 1849 no mention was made of Coupland Beck, Hoff Row or Bleatarn, but the new names of Grange, Heights and Winton appear. The circuit had to report on its preacher, William Fulton. Of him it is stated (*inter alia*) in answer to printed questions that he is 36 years of age; that he is married with three children; that he has travelled for 12½ years; that he is not a tobacco smoker; that he is not in debt; that he is a generally acceptable preacher; that he is not a long preacher; and that he preaches a full, free and present salvation. Among answers to general questions we find that 'Nearly all the places on the plan have been remissioned. We have pressing calls to other places but cannot attend for want of labourers . . .' A letter of eight pages, dated 6th April 1849, is attached to the Report, and in it the Brough members raise organisational questions and claim that they, with over 200 members, could easily support a second minister if one were available. Among the results of their plea was the making of Brough into an independent circuit in 1849.

As with the Baptists and the Wesleyans, so with the Primitive Methodists: not all places responded quickly to their approaches. As far as the Primitive Methodists were concerned Kirkby Stephen provided a real challenge. First visited in 1823, it was not until 1865 that a chapel was erected. Services had previously been held in a small upper room, George Blades and Thomas Rogerson being prominent workers. In 1863/4, during the ministry of James Warnes, there was a period of general revival in the area, and the Kirkby Stephen cause began to flourish. Mr. John Hilton of Mouthlock bought some cottages for £240, and gave a further £50 towards the building of a chapel in their place. Mr. Warnes inspired his flock by word and deed, carting quantities of stone and sand for the building.[57] John Dickinson, a young man who had been converted at Kirkby Stephen on 16th February 1864, was among others who rendered great assistance. In 1905 the building was superseded by a further set of premises comprising chapel, school, hall, and caretaker's house, at a cost of £2,200.

In 1865 James Warnes sent a report to *The Primitive Methodist Magazine*[58] in which he opined that 'our prospects were never so cheering and bright as now'. At Brough, he says, 'the debt four years ago was £49/5/0; now it is reduced to £8'. At Mouthlock 'we have a good work of grace, the society has increased from 14 to 28'. At School House 'we worship in a room rent free, which is often too small for the congregation. God's arm has been made bare; the society has risen from 24 to 44.' As for Newbiggin, 'Here the winter before last we had a blessed work; the spirit of the Lord was poured out in a remarkable manner, young and old, rich and poor, were often seen together seeking pardon through him who died for the world. The society has increased from 30 to 61.' The local impact of national developments is evident in what Warnes has to say of Tebay:

> 'Here our people have worshipped for years in a cottage, but never made any progress. The South Durham Railway having been made through the neighbourhood, the population has considerably increased. We, therefore, three years ago tried to obtain a site to build a chapel on, but could not succeed.
>
> Lately death opened the way . . . The chapel . . . will cost about £135 . . . and it is likely by the time it is opened all the cost will be obtained.'[59]

Not all was plain sailing, however. Although a society of 8 members had been formed at Orton and Bousfield, 'The prospect is not very bright . . .'[60] But over all there was cause for rejoicing, the membership of the circuit having doubled in four years.

An 1867 report to *The Primitive Methodist Magazine* tells

of a further membership increase, of 45. What is especially interesting here is the way in which it becomes clear that socio-economic considerations as well as religious, were beginning to take a hand in relation to the prosperity of the work. In a nutshell, Brough's loss was Tebay's gain. Of Brough it is said that 'in the time of stage coaches the town was a busy and prosperous little place, but the opening of the Lancaster and Carlisle, and South Durham Railways, has put and end here to this mode of travelling. Brough is no longer a noted hostelry . . ., this place, in point of inhabitants and business, is gradually declining.'[61] On the other hand, the arrival of the railway at Tebay, and Primitive Methodism's comparative success with the artisan classes, resulted in the building of a chapel there in 1865. The membership figures are revealing. In the (pre-railway) 1851 return Tebay has 5 members, whilst the return for the year ending 31st December 1884 shows that Tebay, with 81 members, is the strongest society in the circuit, followed by Appleby with 55 members.

Appleby Primitive Methodist chapel (now Jehovah's witnesses).

Primitive Methodism did not reach Appleby until 1867, Isaac Bayliffe being among the pioneers there. A chapel was erected in 1874, and both it and its counterpart at Brough were to suffer from the elements. A new chapel built in Brough in 1877 was struck by lightening and burned down three years later, and early in the present century a burst water main caused flooding which wrecked the Appleby chapel.[62] By 1900 Tebay's membership had fallen to 59. It was still the strongest cause in the circuit, followed by Newbiggin (58), Kirkby Stephen (57), and Appleby (54). Brough appears about half way down the table, with 25 members. The total circuit strength was 149 in 1845; 459 in 1882; and 330 in 1900. It is noteworthy that in none of the Primitive Methodist reports that we have consulted is there any reference to that kind of Anglican hostility which the Wesleyans suffered in the Westmorland Lake District. It should be added that the Hull missionary initiative extended to Penrith and the neighbouring villages. In 1831 these societies were linked to Kendal, and subsequently to Alston. Penrith became an independent circuit in 1876.

Brough (Primitive) Methodist chapel.

One more branch of Methodism remains briefly to be mentioned. A mission conducted in the neighbourhood of Askham by the Bible Christians, under the leadership of a Mrs. Graham, lasted from 1859 to 1862, but bore no permanent denominational fruit.

A further initiative from Scotland comes next to our notice. It will be recalled that James McQuhae of the Associate (Anti-Burgher) Presbytery's chapel in Kendal became an Independent, and left his charge taking a number of sympathisers with him. The remaining Presbyterians struggled on until 1812, when their building was sold. On 8th September 1820 the Associate General (Anti-Burgher) and the Associate (Burgher) Synods united for form the United Secession Church,[63] and it was this body's presbytery of Annan and Carlisle which, in 1823, sent preachers to Kendal with a view to reviving the work there. At first services were held at the Crown Inn, and then, from November 1823, in the old theatre in Woolpack Yard. With the aid of loans the congregation purchased the theatre for £550 and spent nearly as much again in renovating it. Alexander Marshall[64] was ordained to the charge in July 1825. A Sunday School was opened in 1826, and Marshall devoted attention not only to Kendal, but to neighbouring towns and villages as well. In particular, he had a room licensed at Ambleside, and hoped to establish a church there. But in January 1828 there came his untimely death.

Marshall's successor was Robert Wilson, who was ordained at Kendal in December 1828. In 1833 he removed to Greenock. Wilson is chiefly remembered for his anti-Unitarian invective. He delivered a number of provocative lectures in support of the local manifestation of a fairly widespread movement in which Calvinists sought to gain possession of erstwhile trinitarian chapels which had by now become unitarian.[65] In a nutshell the Calvinists held that such properties by virtue of the doctrines originally proclaimed in them, properly belonged to them; the Unitarians countered to the effect that the buildings were theirs by custom and long usage. On one occasion Wilson became so vehement that 'he brought down his hand with such force upon the book before him, as to cause the ledge upon which it rested, to give way, so that he had to hold it in its place, during the remainder of his sermon, and so prevent it from falling upon the head of his precentor, who occupied the desk beneath the pulpit.[66]

Wilson's most vociferous opponent was William Jennings, 'the stoutest and heaviest man, that, perhaps the town of Kendal has ever contained'.[67] A man of parts, Jennings was a wholesaler, an architect, and, inspired by Wilson, a pamphleteer. Originally an Inghamite, he left – or was expelled from – that body as a result of a dispute over baptism in which he unsuccessfully challenged the paedobaptists led by John

Huck. He threw his lot in with James Kay, became unitarian in his views, and eventually accompanied those of Kay's erstwhile congregation who joined the Market Place chapel. During this controversy the Unitarian minister was Edward Hawkes (1833–66)[68] who, besides strongly supporting the Unitarian cause, advocated that of total abstinence (as distinct from temperance). The dissenters received powerful support from George William Wood who, in 1837 became Kendal's first Unitarian M.P.[69] On 19th July 1844 the Dissenters' Chapels Act became law. 'It made retrospective the legalisation of Unitarian doctrine effected in 1813; and it provided that, so far as trusts did not specify doctrines, twenty-five years' tenure was enough to legitimate existing doctrinal usage.'[70]

Meanwhile, in the north-east of the county the Baptist advance was under way, and to this we now turn.[71] On 21st June 1827 the Baptist chapel at Middleton in Teesdale was opened by Dr. Steadman and Mr. Godwin of Horton College, Bradford. The origins of this cause lie in the movements of the Baptist James Goodburn, a blacksmith, who, together with some of his fellow church members, moved from Hamsterley to Middleton on the opening there of the new mines of the London Lead Company. In time Goodburn influenced the governor of the mine, Robert Stagg, and his family, to become Baptists, and Stagg approached David Douglas, Hamsterley's minister, for advice on the establishment of a cause at Middleton. For a time the new church was served by student supplies from Bradford, Charles Hill Roe among them. On 6th May 1828 a church of 16 members was formed, and a call was addressed to Mr. Roe. On the following day he was ordained and inducted to the Middleton pastorate.[72]

The Baptist interest prospered, and in 1832 Mr. James Sneath was appointed missioner to Teesdale by the Baptist Home Missionary Society.[73] At first he had a special responsibility for the work at Forest, where on 6th June 1834 a chapel and cottage were opened, Mr. Stagg once again being a principal benefactor. Meanwhile in 1830 some Baptists at Brough appealed for help to their Middleton brethren, and it seems that for a time a Mr. Tapscot served them as missionary. Douglas refers to him as being ordained and inducted at

South Shields on 2nd December 1832, on the death of Mr. Angus.[74] In 1831 Mr. Swale, then missionary at Forest, preached at Brough, and eventually Mr. Harvey, a student from Bradford, was sent as missioner to Brough, Charles Roe being instrumental in securing this appointment. Roe enlisted the financial support of the Yorkshire Itinerant Society (£20 p.a.) and the Baptist Home Missionary Society (£10 p.a.); and Mr. Benjamin Goodman of Leeds was a further benefactor. On 16th March 1834 Philip Robinson and Joseph Yare journeyed to Middleton in Teesdale and became the first Brough men to be baptised. Their example was followed by others, and a church of seven members was formed on 8th June 1834.[75]

James Sneath of Forest was ordained at Brough on 8th September 1835. He worked hard, and soon had meetings established at a number of villages and hamlets in the surrounding area. Conditions were physically arduous; in some places there was churchly and other opposition; and in material terms the lot of Sneath and his fellow ministers left much to be desired. At a committee meeting of the Home Missionary Society held on 7th July 1837 it was 'Resolved that a gratuity of £5 be forwarded to Mr. Sneath and that our Secretary enquire of Mr. Robinson the Deacon whether the church at Brough will agree to collect more towards Mr. Sneath's salary for if not we must tho' reluctantly withdraw our grant'.[76] Again, in a letter to Mr. Bartlett dated 17th February 1910 Mr. R. Jackson recalls a minister who continued with his trade as a shoemaker until he could bear the financial strain of working among the Westmorland Baptists no longer. 'Ministers' he writes, 'were starved into debt', and to this the brevity of many of the pastorates in the area must be attributed. Despite all, Douglas is able to record a membership of 100 at Brough in 1845, and a Sunday School of 30 children. The minister at the time was J. J. Osborne. As for the district at large, an 1843 preaching plan for the Westmorland Baptist Mission gives the names of the minister (J. J. Osborn) and twelve lay preachers, and shows stations at Brough, Winton, Kirkby Stephen, Crosby Garrett, Waitby, Waterhouses, Whygill Head, Raisbeck, Orton, Asby, Drybeck, Hoff, Crackenthorpe and Kirkby Thore. An impressive list indeed, especially considering that both Wesleyan and Primitive Methodists were also active in the neighbourhood.

At first the Brough church had no settled home, but eventually Philip Robinson, manager of the Augill Lead Mines, was instrumental in having a chapel built. In 1848 Brough and Asby were designated district churches, with the responsibility of holding church meetings and arranging the ordinances for their respective localities. Sadly, difficulties ensued at Brough – apparently in connection with a mortgage, since creditors siezed the chapel. An entry in the Church Minute Book records that early in 1849 'the Church at Brough was dissolved under peculiar circumstances and re-formed'. In the following year a new chapel was built, the Revd. William Fawcett preaching the opening sermons. The minister at the time was the Revd. James Kay, and for a while the cause flourished. Brough Baptists gained much local publicity when the Hon. and Revd. Baptist Noel, who, disquieted with things Anglican had become a Baptist in 1849, preached in their chapel c.1852.[77] In 1859 the Revd. H. Dunn became pastor, and whereas at first all was well, he shortly adopted and began to propagate Christadelphian views. The result of this was that church life at both Brough and Winton was seriously disturbed. The arrival in 1865 of the Revd. Alex. Grant from college in Glasgow did much to stem the tide, and during his ministry the debts outstanding on some of the chapels was cleared. From an entry by Grant in the earliest extant Minute Book (1865) we can gather something of the state and relationships of the causes in his time:

> 'Towards the end of July I have a cordial and unanimous invitation from the Church at Brough, Winton and Great Asby to become their Pastor, at the same time a letter from the Church at Crosby Garrett inviting me to become Co-pastor with Mr. Fawcett, both which I accepted and began my labours as pastor of the one Church and Co-Pastor of the other on the 12th of August.
>
> The Church having been long destitute of regular pastoral supervision, the Church books appear to have been partly mislaid and all that can clearly be made out is that the brethren at these stations (Brough, Winton, Asby) form *one* Church, so far as to unite under care of and com-

> municate to the support of one Pastor; yet so distinct as to be able to attend to the Lord's Supper, manage the smaller details of business and exercise Christian discipline at each of the stations. That the Church consists of, and communion is restricted to baptized believers – and that the weightier matters of business are managed by delegates from the several stations who meet once every three months to examine accounts and consult as to the best means of promoting the peace and growth of the Church.'

After Mr. Fawcett's departure from Crosby Garrett in 1873 the cause there became fully a part of the one Westmorland Baptist church. Mr. Grant left the district in 1871, and after various attempts to inject life into the Brough station it was closed in 1911, a small outstanding debt being cleared by the group in 1915.

Among the early stations was that at Raisbeck. Kent records that in 1839 Mr. and Mrs. Barnard Hoodleston opened their house for meetings, and it was there, under the ministry of James Sneath, that John Burra of Raisbeck was converted. He married in 1845, and in 1848 he opened his new home at Kelleth for worship. Services were held there for over fifty years, and in due time John's son Abraham became owner of the house, and Secretary and Treasurer of the Westmorland Baptist Group.

We may be reasonably confident that the Whygill Head church was formed on 5th January 1840. A minute quoted by Kent states that on that day a church of the Particular Baptist denomination was constituted 'in the presence of John Brame, agent of the Baptist Home Missionary Society . . . and Isaac Ebdell, one of the deacons . . . at Brough'. Eleven members were admitted to the roll 'by giving and receiving of hands': Mary Jackson, Mary Dent, George Jordan, John Jackson, John Stewardson, John Penrith, Jane Jackson, Richard Taylor, Mary Burra, Ellen Atkinson and Mary Brunskill. John Jackson and John Stewardson were appointed deacons. All those named had previously been baptised – almost certainly at Brough. (The minute from which these particulars are extracted appears decisive, though a ms. letter states that Mr. Greenwood formed the Whygill Head church in 1839; and another notes that 1839 is given as the date of formation in one minute book, and 1840 in another.) By 1842 there were 35 members on the church roll, and they were drawn from a wide area. The building of a chapel was contemplated, but it was never undertaken. Services were, however, held at Whygill Head until 1899, by which time many of the older members had died or removed, and nonconformity was represented in the area by the new Congregational church at Little Asby.

It is quite possible that, as some sources state, Mr. Greenwood of Crosby Garrett was intimately associated with the Whygill Head church. What is absolutely beyond question is that he was a tower of strength to the Baptist movement in his own village. Crosby Garrett had long been associated with the nonconformist cause. It is thought that from the time of Christopher Jackson dissenting services were held there. Prominent among the nonconforming families were the Richardsons. Colonel Richard Richardson was party to the Kaber Rigg Plot, and went to ground after its failure. Joseph Richardson had his home, Mossgill House, licensed for worship on 7th October 1754,[78] and subsequently a chapel (originally Independent, and with close links with that at Ravenstonedale) was made out of converted farm buildings adjoining the house. Nicolson and Burn record the existence of nine dissenting families in Crosby Garrett in 1777.

Crosby Garrett Baptist chapel.

In 1804 Nancy Richardson of Mossgill House, Ravenstonedale, one of the Richardsons of Crosby Garrett, married George Greenwood of Hull. A merchant and ship owner, he was an ardent Baptist lay preacher. He and his new wife came to live at Crosby Garrett, and were responsible for the enlargement of the chapel. Baptist influence increased among the members, and eventually a Baptist church of fourteen members was formed comprising, George Greenwood, Thomas Brunskill, John Penrith, Mary Penrith, Thomas Bolt, William Nicholson, Sarah Nicholson, John Jackson, George Jackson, G. Green sen., G. Green jnr., Sarah Thompson, Deborah Thompson and Mary Thompson.[79] Until 1856 both the Independents and the Baptists used the chapel, the Ravenstonedale minister conducting services for the former on alternate Sundays. In time the Independents declined, while the Baptists received a considerable access of strength on the arrival in the village in 1856 of the Revd. William Fawcett, a grandson of John Fawcett D.D., who wrote the hymn, 'Blest be the tie that binds'. Of independent means, he came to reside at Mossgill House on his marriage to Deborah Greenwood, George's daughter. He worked *gratis,* was highly regarded as a preacher, and his generosity was widely known. In 1859, during a period of revival under his ministry, seventeed believers were baptised, eleven in Potts Beck, a stream about a mile from the village, and the remainder at Brough. Mr. Fawcett preached his farewell sermon on 19th October 1873. On the following day at a farewell meeting, he was presented with his portrait in oils, and with an inscribed gold watch. Miss Fawcett received an inscribed walnut devonport. The sum of £60 had been subscibed by friends. Mr. Fawcett died at Florence on 17th December 1874, aged 75.

We have already referred to Isaac Ebdell's association with the cause at Whygill Head in 1840. By that time he had already pioneered in his home village of Winton. Originally a member of the Kirkby Stephen Independent church, he responded to an approach of the Brough Baptists to provide a venue for occasional services at Winton. Ebdell agreed to allow the Baptists the use of his kitchen, provided that no reference should be made in services there to believers' baptism. The agreement was kept by the Baptists, but on one occasion the local Congregational minister preached a sermon in defence of paedobaptism. This prompted Ebdell to study the matter for himself, and he concluded in favour of the Baptist position. On a bitterly cold winter's day he and his wife, and two of his wife's sisters, travelled to Brough to be baptised. The ice on Brough beck had to be broken before the ordinance could be performed, but the converts were undeterred. The Church Minute Book records the death of Mr. Ebdell on 27th November 1868, and states that he was 'for nearly thirty-two years a consistent, earnest and active member of the church'. This suggests a date in the mid 1830's for the formation of the Winton Baptist Church. Certainly Winton appears on a preaching plan for 1842. Ebdell's kitchen was soon too small for the services, so he converted another part of his premises. Eventually, he gave some land on which a chapel was erected in 1863. Mr. Fawcett threw his financial weight behind the venture, and the total cost of chapel and school was £248/4/6.

William Fawcett also did much to further the Baptist cause at Great Asby. The roots of the work here go back to the prolific labours of James Sneath. The story goes that he overheard a conversation between the Rector of Asby and the ostler of a public house in Brough, which persuaded him that the spiritual needs of Asby were being none too well met. Sneath went to Asby and encouraged Mr. Robert Yare Fairer, grandfather of Mrs. Isaac Ebdell, to open his house for worship. Mr. Fairer later fitted up a chapel at his own expense,

Great Asby Baptist chapel.

and at times over a hundred people crowded into it. In 1862 the present chapel was built at a cost of £200, and the opening address was delivered by the Revd. Dr. Pattinson, then of Middleton in Teesdale and subsequently of Harvard University. In 1893 a schoolroom was added at a cost of £70.

Bulmer (1885) notes that at Shap the Baptists have a meeting room 'erected about sixteen years ago, chiefly through the efforts of Miss Elizabeth Wilson, of Kendal, now a missionary among the Chinese'.[80] It was evidently abandoned many years ago. The government Register of 1882 makes no reference to it, though mention is made of a Shap group 'who object to be designated'. Since those of a unitarian persuasion sometimes employed this description it may be that the Shap Baptists were in the General rather than the Particular Baptist tradition, the former being more susceptible to unitarian influence than the latter. This remains an hypothesis which cannot be substantiated, since there are no records which would associate the Shap Baptists with the undesignated chapel. Nor is there any evidence that the Shap Baptists had fellowship with their brethren over the hills, and the likelihood is that they did not.

As we saw earlier, attempts were made to establish the Baptist cause in Kirkby Stephen at the end of the eighteenth century, but the struggling congregation soon failed. Not even the energies of James Sneath could place things on a firm footing there. Although Kirkby Stephen was a preaching station in his day it was not until 1885, during the ministry of G. McDonald, that a new initiative was taken. At first services were held in an inconvenient upper room in a back yard, but on 15th October 1890 Dr. Landels of Edinburgh opened a new chapel which had cost £827/4/8½. The site had been given by Mrs. Jackson, widow of John Jackson of Little Asby; and through the generosity of another stalwart supporter, Miss Emma E. Thompson, a manse was obtained for the group minister.

In the United Methodists of the Appleby circuit we have Westmorland's only long-standing representatives of the most radical variety of Methodism.[81] (A cause at Kendal, which returned 31 members in 1837 does not appear in the *Minutes* of the Wesleyan Association after 1839). It was in 1835 that in common with some 20,000 like-minded methodists from various parts of the country, a group in the Appleby area seceded from the Wesleyans and formed the Wesleyan Association, whose leader was Dr. Samuel Warren. Ostensibly it was the 1835 Methodist Conference dispute over the propriety or otherwise of establishing a theological institution which prompted the secession (or, in some cases, the expulsion) of so many members of the Methodist fold. Not far below the surface, however, was increasing dismay at the autocratic ways of Conference – especially as represented by Dr. Jabez Bunting – and a growing conviction that a form of Methodist church government which allowed a much fuller practical expression of the doctrine of the priesthood of all beleivers was an urgent necessity. It is possible that the quest of democracy, very much to the fore in the age of the Reform Bill, played its part in moulding secession opinion. On the other hand, it should be remembered that the Methodism of the day was *generally* conservative, and that politically inspired agitators were few in Wesleyan ranks. There was almost certainly a theological, rather than a political motive behind the resolution passed at the first Conference of the Wesleyan Association to the effect that it is 'inexpedient that the term "Reverend" should be used in connexion with any preacher in the Association'.[82] The motives of the seceders were similar to those which had inspired the founders of the Protestant Methodists in 1827 (when the *ostensible* cause of the breach was the hostility of the protesters to the installation of an organ in Brunswick Chapel, Leeds). These two bodies came together between 1837–9. A much larger secession, comprising 100,000 members, occurred in 1849 when James Everett, Samuel Dunn and William Griffith formed the Wesleyan Reformers on their expulsion from the parent body whose procedures they could not conscientiously approve. The Reformers and the Association united in 1857 to form the United Methodist Free Churches. This body united with the Methodist New Connexion (founded on the secession of Alexander Kilham and his supporters from the Wesleyans in 1797) and the Bible Christians (founded in 1815 on the Devon–Cornwall borders by William O'Bryan) in 1907. Whereas Kilham's objectives generally accorded with those later to be sought by the Protestant Methodists, Warren, and the Reformers, those of the Bible Christians were evangelistic. The latter body, if generalisation may be permitted, resembled the Primitive Methodists in ethos and the New Connexion Methodists in government.

Turning to the introduction of the Wesleyan Association into Westmorland we come at once upon the name of John Dent (12.9.1792–2.12.1871) of Bolton near Appleby.[83] Brought up an Anglican, he became a Methodist in the year 1817. His father and a few older members of the family had by then been Methodists for some time, the Revd. George Smith of the Kirkby Stephen Wesleyan circuit having introduced Methodism into Bolton c.1803. Mr. Dent senior allowed preaching services in his house, and there they continued, even after his death in 1816, until a small chapel was built in 1818. By now John Dent was a class leader and a local preacher. In 1824 he married the like-minded Agnes Crosby, and together they laboured in the Wesleyan cause until 1835. Then, as the *Nicholson ms.* has it, 'the doings of the Conference causes him to make a stand against what he [i.e. John Dent] was convinced was tyranny springing up in Methodism'. He attended a meeting of dissatisfied Wesleyans in Sheffield in 1835, and in the following year threw his lot in with Dr. Warren. The Bolton members unanimously supported Dent and, since the Bolton chapel was vested with the Wesleyans, he opened a room in his house for services. For four years the chapel was unused, except for a Sunday School conducted by the seceders. After arduous negotiations the building was transferred to the Wesleyan Association. In 1926 it was superseded by a new chapel built by the United Methodists.[84]

Meanwhile at Kirkby Thore the Crosby family, who had given the land of which the Wesleyan chapel of 1828 stood, and who had liberally supported the cause there, seceded to the Association. Others joined them, but the secession here was not unanimous. Indeed, the membership was almost evenly divided. At first the two parties used the chapel alternatively, but when in 1849 further troubles shook the Conference, local friction ensued. Though the Crosbys claimed the chapel – and fought for it at Appleby assizes – the building was securely in Wesleyan hands. Eventually, in 1859 the (by now) United Methodist Free Church members erected their own building under the leadership of James and Samuel Crosby.

The seceders brought great enthusiasm to their work, and the Wesleyan Association Circuit Book[85] records the following station and membership details as at the first quarter day held at Appleby on 21st December 1836: Appleby (17); Bolton (17); Brampton (4); Brough (9); Dufton (–); Kirkby Thore (25); Murton (10); Peaselands (6); Warcop (7); Penrith (Cumberland) (16); making a total of 111. In addition there are 7 members on trial. The total income for the quarter was £11/2/0, of which Kirkby Thore provided the largest sum, £3/2/6. If we compare the above information with that provided by the first Wesleyan Quarterly Schedule for 1837 we find that the Wesleyans were outnumbered by the seceders at Appleby (10); Kirkby Thore (16); and Bolton (–); but that the Wesleyans remained stronger at Brough (30); Dufton (39); Murton (30); and Warcop (17).

Appleby United Methodist chapel (now a Youth Centre)

The Association's ministers resided at Appleby, the first of them being the Revd. William Mackenney (1836–8). He was born in Derby on 4th December 1799; he was converted in 1818, became a local preacher in 1819, and was expelled by the Wesleyans in 1832. After serving as an Arminian Methodist minister in Derby he joined the Wesleyan Association, and Appleby was his first charge under that body. He served a second time at Appleby (1844–6), and died at Barnstaple on 27th June 1884.[86] In 1840 the circuit published a report in which it was stated that their sense of geographical isolation from their brethren notwithstanding, the members were holding their own.[87] But some of the early enthusiasm waned. Certainly the seventeenth meeting of the Wesleyan Methodist Association held at Manchester in 1852 deemed it appropriate to resolve that 'the Assembly judges Appleby circuit able to pay the balance of Brother Steele's salary, and hopes it will do so before he leaves'.[88]

A Special Schedule of the United Methodist Free Churches for 1881 provides the following information as to the stations, and as to the date and cost of the erection or purchase of the chapels: Appleby (1870 : £800); Colby (1874 : £200); Maulds Meaburn (1878 : £245); Murton (1841 : £100); Warcop (1844 : £120); Sandford (1848 : £90); Bolton (1818 : –); Kirkby Thore (1851 : £150); Asby (1859 : £140). Maulds Meaburn alone is shown as having an outstanding debt (of £56) on the building, but this means that the members there had raised almost £200 in about three years. It is further stated that the Bolton chapel, originally Wesleyan, has not been re-certified, and that the Asby deed makes no denominational specification.

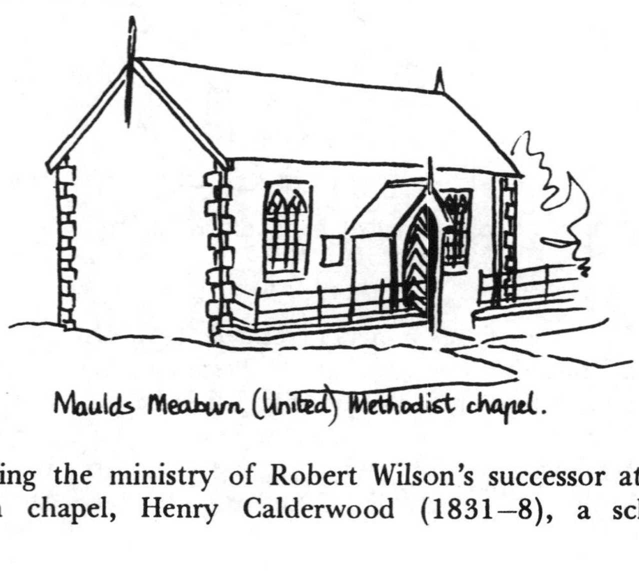

Maulds Meaburn (United) Methodist chapel.

During the ministry of Robert Wilson's successor at the Scotch chapel, Henry Calderwood (1831–8), a schism occurred amongst the Kendal Friends which led initially to the strengthening of the Presbyterian cause, and subsequently to the establishment of a Brethren assembly in the town. It appears that the issue was doctrinal, and parallel with that in America between evangelical Friends on the one hand, and their rationalistic, unitarian Hicksite brethren on the other. The evangelical Quaker Isaac Crewdson of Kendal and Manchester, a prominent banker and industrialist, published *A Beacon to the Society of Friends* in 1835. In it he contrasted his own views with those of the Hicksites. At the heart of the matter was the question of authority. What is the Bible, and how is its authority to be squared with the individual's inward light?[89] For his part Crewdson believed that Friends had grossly neglected the scriptures. After a period as a quietist, he underwent an evangelical conversion experience which had been prompted by his realisation of the importance of the doctrine of the atonement. Bible study also led him to question Quaker views concerning female ministry and birthright membership, and to advocate the sacraments of believers' baptism and the Lord's Supper. In 1836 he and his brother-in-law, William Boulton, resigned from the Manchester meeting, taking their sympathisers with them. The Beaconites, as they were known, launched a magazine, *The Inquirer.* It reported 'the first occasion of public baptism amongst the Evangelical Friends' at which Crewdson presided and Boulton prayed,[90] and carried regular news of Beaconite progress.

In 1837 the Westmorland Quarterly Meeting sought the advice of the London Yearly Meeting on the question whether or not Friends should partake of sacraments. Lengthy discussion ensued – not least as to whether the Westmorland query *was* a query or a proposal – and in the end it was resolved to return the proposition whence it had come.[91] The upshot was that despite the opposition of the notable evangelical Quaker, Anna Braithwaite, about 100 Kendal Friends resigned from the meeting. A group of Evangelical Friends appears to have been meeting in the town as late as 1862; others joined the Scotch Chapel. They were not long in their new home, for about 1837 they left it to form a Brethren assembly. With the Crewdsons went their banking partner, E. W. Wakefield.[92] At first they met in a room in the Whitehall on Sundays, and in a warehouse on weekdays, but on 10th October 1857 *The Kendal Mercury* was able to report that the Brethren had opened a 'very elegant and commodious place of worship' in Stramongate. At this time another group of Brethren who seceded from the Inghamite chapel shortly after *their* new building (superseding the one of 1758) was opened in 1844, amalgamated with the original group. This necessitated the doubling in size of the Sand Area meeting room in January 1863. The Kendal Brethren opened a new church in Parr Street on 23rd May 1971.

Brethren church, Kendal.

As for the remainder of the county, we may note that at Bowness Brethren work began c.1836, and the present hall was made out of buildings in Bank Terrace c.1851. An important Brethren conference on the exclusive-open issue was held at Windermere in 1891.[93] As for Kirkby Stephen, Bulmer (1885) states that the Brethren began to hold services in Melbecks Meeting Room 'some seven years ago',[94] and this is confirmed by local enquiries. However, this meeting does not appear in the 1882 government Return. Bulmer also mentions Brethren baptisms by immersion in the nearby river, and Gospel Services conducted by the Brethren in the Midland Station Booking Hall. The fourth surviving Brethren assembly in Westmorland is that at Ambleside. It began as a mission at some time before 1900, and now meets in a rented house. At the turn of the century there was a Brethren assembly at Shap, but it was discontinued many years ago.

As for the continuing Friends, we find them developing a characteristic variety of the nonconformist conscience, as witness their opposition to a theatre in Kendal;[95] the philanthropic and social concern of such Friends as Mrs. Hannah Wilson, Miss Jane Whitwell and Mrs. D. Crewdson;[96] and the Quaker Sunday School which, after some false starts from 1830, became firmly established in Kendal in 1859.[97] Stramongate School continued, with varying degrees of success, to provide a broadly-based education. The Kendal Preparative Meeting of 23rd December 1810 took the first steps towards the introduction of girls into the school – despite the opposition of headmaster Dalton. The tenure of Henry Thompson as headmaster (1860–78) was among the stablest in the century, and during his time the school became a public boarding school.

Friends' meeting house (1816), Kendal.

Like their fellows in other parts of the country, some nineteenth century Westmorland Quakers became prominent in business. The Wakefields of Kendal were bankers – though, as we have seen, E. W. Wakefield subsequently joined the Brethren. From the *Nicholson ms.* we learn that the Wakefields' banknotes carried an engraving of a rock and a sycamore tree to be found on Brooks Hall Estate, Appleby. Again, Quakers from Kendal and Darlington were to the fore in promoting the South Durham and Eden Valley railway lines. These made a considerable impact upon, and provided opportunities of employment within, the Kirkby Stephen area. The growth of Tebay was a further visible result of the advent of the railway.

For the most part Quaker meetings were in a state of flux. The meeting at Underbarrow (renamed Crook before 1699) closed in 1835, whilst that at Preston Patrick closed in 1852, and reopened in 1874. The cause at Grayrigg survived until 1841, was revived in 1896, and finally closed in 1952. A meeting at Mislet, Windermere, continued until 1822, its meeting house subsequently being demolished in 1841. Its contemporary at Tirril, where a meeting house had been opened in 1733, closed down in 1862. About 1800 the old Strickland meeting removed to Morland, a meeting house being opened there in 1806 and closed in 1903.

Reference to yet another schism, that involving John Guthrie of the Scotch chapel, will bring our account of nineteenth century developments to a close. A native of Milnathort, Kinross-shire, Guthrie entered the University of Edinburgh in November 1831.[98] There he renewed contact with James Morison, whom he had met when the latter paid a visit to a cousin in Milnathort a year before. Guthrie took his M.A. in the spring of 1835, and had been a member of the Divinity Hall of the United Secession Church since August 1834. The young man was greatly impressed by a passage in Dr. John Brown's inaugural address, in which the practice of 'first making creeds and confessions ostensibly in defence of Bible truths and then of committing the shameless idolatry of falling down and worshipping them, to the disparagement of the Word of God'[99] was eloquently denounced. Licensed by the Dunfermline presbytery in the spring of 1838, Guthrie settled at Kendal, within the Lancashire presbytery of his church, and was ordained on 25th February, 1839.

Guthrie maintained contact with James Morison, and found himself in sympathy with the latter's opposition to the Calvinistic doctrine of limited atonement. It should be made clear that neither Morison nor Guthrie denied that salvation is of grace; nor did they assert that man is competent to save himself. But they moved from the concept of God's electing grace as being a matter of eternal decree, to the view that election is a temporal matter, and that atonement having been made once and for all, the Holy Spirit enables the sinner to place his trust in Christ as all-sufficient Saviour. Negatively, they were opposed to the Calvinist's apparent acquiescense in capricious favouritism on the part of the Almighty.

When Morison was called to answer charges at the Synod of June 1841, Guthrie, through ignorance of the Synod's procedures, was not able to support him publicly, or to speak against his suspension from the ministry – on which course Synod determined. Subsequently, however, and with the cordial support of the Kendal session, he presented a memorial to the 1842 Synod, in which a protest was lodged against a further deliberation of the previous year's Synod, namely, that whereby 'all ministers and preachers of this church must consider themselves prohibited from preaching for Mr. Morison, or employing him in any of their pulpit ministrations'.[100] Guthrie spoke to his memorial, but the Synod, having already, during the first week of its session, deposed James Morison's sympathetic father, Robert, of Bathgate, was in no mood to be persuaded.

On returning to Kendal, Guthrie was under obligation to read his congregation an official paper entitled, *Doctrinal Errors Condemned by the United Associate Synod of 1842.* He not only read it, he criticised it and, since ill health prevented his attendance, he sent written objections to the Lancashire presbytery meeting at Hallfold, Rochdale. Fuel was added to the fire when Guthrie, at Sir Wilfrid Lawson's behest, preached during an evangelistic campaign at Maryport. Among other preachers taking part was James Morison. Although these meetings were non-sectarian, and despite the fact that Guthrie's preaching on 12th October did not take place during the 'canonical hours' of a Sunday, the presbytery of Annan and Carlisle shortly wrote to him complaining that he had been ministerially associated with Morison. The complaint was forwarded to the clerk of the Lancashire presbytery, but no immediate action was taken in view of Guthrie's continued indisposition.

Guthrie took pains to make his position clear to the members of his congregation – not indeed by way of eliciting their personal support, but in the interests of gospel truth as he conceived it. Most, though not all, were persuaded, and some of those who were not were 'as rank Antinomians as ever breathed and boasted'.[101] As well as providing verbal explanations, Guthrie took up his fluent pen. Prior to the 1843 Synod he published *New Views – True Views,* the preface to which is dated 25th February 1843. Two further pamphlets followed. He gave his views upon the proceedings of Synod, and he took a local Calvinist, Mr. J. E. Howard, to task.[102]

At the 1843 Synod Guthrie, after speaking in support of the suspended A. C. Rutherford of Falkirk, was himself suspended and then deposed – unconstitutionally, as he thought.[103] He wrote to the Kendal church, placing himself in their hands, and was warmly invited to return to their midst. A number of members of another church in Kendal also met, and wrote to Guthrie expressing their desire that he would return to the town, and promising to throw their lot in with him. Whilst awaiting the reply of his congregation, Guthrie stayed at Kilmarnock, the scene of James Morison's ministry, and there between 16th–18th May 1843 the Morisons, Rutherford, Guthrie, evangelist Alex Forsyth, and a number of representative elders met together, and the Evangelical Union was formed.[104] Guthrie was to serve this body as President on two occasions (1846 and 1854), as Secretary (1843–44), and as theological tutor.

Guthrie returned to Kendal, and about 100 church members seceded from the Woolpack Yard church with him, leaving a remnant of 30.[105] The entire Sunday School was on his side, and its work was continued without interruption in the Oddfellows Hall. Meanwhile steps were taken towards the erection of Zion chapel.[106] The following is a copy of the foundation Statement, dated 24th January 1844, clause IV of the doctrinal section being the operative one:

Statement of Doctrine

I. That the Scriptures of the Old and New Testament are given by inspiration of God, and are the only rule of faith and practice.

II. That God is revealed in the Scriptures as the Father, Son, and Holy Spirit; and that to each are attributable the same divine properties and perfections.

III. That the first Man disobeyed the Divine command, fell from his state of innocence and purity, and involved all his Posterity in the consequences of that fall; that, therefore, all mankind are born in sin, and that a fatal inclination to moral evil, utterly incurable by human means, is inherent in every descendant of Adam.

IV. That the Son of God, by whom the worlds were created, and by whom all things consist, was made flesh, and died upon the Cross, a propitiation for the sins of the whole world, thus throwing open the door of mercy to all men; that through His perfect righteousness and atoning sacrifice, all, who are led by the Holy Spirit to repent and believe in Him, are delivered from condemnation, and, being, justified by faith, have peace with God, are made heirs of eternal life, and receive the gift of the Holy Spirit to sanctify them wholly; that being thus made alive unto God by a new creation in Christ Jesus unto good works, the Believer delights in the Holy Law of God, takes it as his rule of duty, and seeks to grow in grace, and in the knowledge of our Lord and Saviour Jesus Christ.

Statement of Church Order, &c.

I. No meeting of the Church shall be valid, when held for purposes affecting the constitution of the Church, the election, character, qualifications, or deposition, of a Minister, Trustees, or those holding office in the Church, except notice of such Meeting, stating the object for which it is required, be given to the Church at the close of one of the public services on four Sabbaths preceding the day on which such meeting may be held.

II. In meetings for appointing Committees, for managing the secular affairs of the Church, or for the admission of Members by vote, should such a plan at any time be adopted, a majority of the Members present shall be necessary and sufficient to decide, provided the Meeting has been duly intimated to the Church at the close of the public service on the previous Sabbath.

III. The Minister, or some one holding office in the Church, shall be required to call a Church Meeting, whenever one-fourth of the whole number of Members on the roll-book at the time, present a requisition to that effect.

IV. A majority of the whole number of Members of the church, whose names have been on the roll-book as Members six months previous to such Meeting of the Church, shall be necessary and sufficient to carry any question put to vote, affecting the constitution of the Church; the character or qualifications of a Minister, or the deposition of a Minister from all connection with the Church and Place of Worship; or the election, character, qualifications, or deposition, of Trustees, or those holding office in the Church; two-thirds of such number shall be necessary and sufficient to carry the election of a Minister.

V. The number of Trustees, in whom the Chapel and Premises shall be wholly vested, shall be nine; and whenever their number shall be reduced to three, an appointment shall be made of as many as may be necessary to make up the whole number to nine; and in all meetings of the Trustees, three, or more, shall constitute a quorum.

VI. None shall be eligible to hold the office of Trustee, but such as are enrolled Members of the Church; and Trustees shall hold office only as long as they continue Members of the Church.

VII. At no time shall the Trustees mortgage, or otherwise encumber, the Chapel and Premises to an amount exceeding £350.

VIII. Whenever the Church ceases to pay the interest of any debt upon the Premises, or to defray the necessary expenses of keeping up and continuing regular Public Worship in the place, a majority of the Trustees shall have power to sell any part, or the whole of the Premises; and the amount received at such sale, after deducting all reasonable expenses, shall be appropriated in such manner as a majority of the Members of the Church then upon the roll-book may decide;– always providing that it be given to some religious object in accordance with the terms of the Trust Deed.

In view of the last clause here a letter which Guthrie addressed to the Committee of Zion Chapel c.1846 is not without interest. He here takes upon himself the 'difficult, delicate and dangerous task' of speaking out on matters financial. He argues that 'A church in our position should do more than others, first, for the truth's sake, which is seldom to be found so unfettered; and second, from the difficulties of our separate and independent position'. Like many before and since, Guthrie draws comparisons:

> 'I am not wishing to forget the pressure of the times, nor my liability to mistake in some of my data. Nor do I know, or wish to know, what share of the blame lies at the door of individuals. All that I know is two or three general data which enable me to ascertain with arithmetical certainty how much 125 members contribute among them. If my data be correct, it turns out that these 125 – comprising a good many in circumstances above that of operatives – are contributing at the rate of 2d. a week, i.e. they are not giving more than one half, nor even than one third of what many a poor man with a large family is able to spend on *tobacco*'.

He goes on to say that he does not wish the church to be 'burdened by my support, and will take what they have to give', but if the great body of the members fail to make a realistic financial contribution, 'I must simply interpret the symptoms and act accordingly'. A few wealthy members gave generously, but many were not pulling their weight.

Zion, Kendal (now U.R.C.).

For all that, the Zion members had opened their new chapel on 16th October 1844, at a cost of £1,250, and in later years Guthrie was able to write: 'I may only add that, during all our trials and critical vicissitudes as a church, we never dropped one of our extra missionary and other contributions; and that these were never larger than at the very time we were going deep into our pockets for the new chapel'.[107]

In November 1848 Guthrie left Kendal for Glasgow, where he was to lead a congregation of but 22 members which eventually blossomed as North Dundas Street church. Although his salary declined by two-thirds on making the move, the conduct of his professorial duties was facilitated. Fergus Ferguson summed up Guthrie the man as follows:

> 'Others of our leaders may awe by their earnestness, and force a place for themselves, among eminent contemporaries, by their perseverance and their power; but [Guthrie] woos and wins by his love and his catholicity of spirit. Too large-hearted for any sect, he has a greater number of clerical friends out of our communion than in it; while his fame, as a writer on church government and Nonconformity, and also as a Christian poet, has been widely spread abroad.'[108]

It remains only to add that as the years passed, Zion grew closer to organised Congregationalism, and during the ministry of James Groat (1907–19)[109] the fellowship became formally associated with that body.

Most of those who remained at the Scotch Chapel after the departure of Guthrie and his supporters were elderly and infirm. When the seceders made a bid of £450 for the property, it was only through the generosity of Mr. George Smith, an elder of the congregation at Mount Pleasant, Liverpool, that the Secession Church was able to retain it. On 13th August 1845, after a period of eighteen months as missionary in Kendal, the Revd. John Inglis was ordained to the ministry at the Scotch Chapel. In 1847 the Secession and Relief Churches united, and the Scotch Chapel became Kendal's United Presbyterian cause. Mr. Inglis resigned owing to ill health on 19th January 1858, and was succeeded by the Revd. Hugh

Wallace, who was ordained on 29th March 1859.[110] In June 1894 the congregation was received into the Carlisle Presbytery of the Presbyterian Church of England, and a new building, named St. John's, was opened in Sandes Avenue in April 1897.

Largely as a result of evangelical zeal, but truth to tell, partly as a consequence of (sometimes perversely attractive) schism, nonconformity was as strong as it has ever been across Westmorland as a whole at the turn of the nineteenth century.

St. John's Presbyterian chapel (now U.R.C.) Kendal.

V – RETROSPECT, COMPARISONS AND CONTRASTS

We have seen that George Fox found a ready-made audience of Seekers when he arrived in Westmorland. These quickly acknowledged him as leader, and the Society of Friends was soon under way in the county. The ejected ministers of Westmorland made some slight impact within the county, but the success of the Friends and the *general* conservatism of the gentry impeded the progress of Old Dissent. After the Toleration Act the rural dissenting causes in Westmorland gradually declined and, partly by reason of geographical isolation, they suffered a double portion of pre-evangelical-revival lethargy. In numerical terms the urban Presbyterian congregation of Kendal fared better. We have noted Nicholson and Axon's doubt as to whether the members of this cause were ever explicitly trinitarian, and we have traced their movement, in keeping with *avant garde* theological fashion of the early eighteenth century, towards an avowedly unitarian position. The Baptists were not organised in the county prior to the Evangelical Awakening, but once that occurred they advanced (though never into the Lake District), as did the Congregationalists. The same revival brought the Methodists into the area. Whereas Fox had found the Seekers eager to join him, the Inghamites did not immediately turn to Wesley. Moreover, in some areas, notably the Lake District, Anglican resentment against 'enthusiasm', and the general apathy of the people, ran high and hindered Wesleyan progress. The Wesleyans' early successes were due quite as much to initiatives from within the county – such as that taken by the Brunskills of Winton – as to the itinerant ministry of Wesley himself.

Both the Baptist and the stronger part of the Primitive Methodist entry into the county was by the doorway of Brough. But whereas the Baptist thrust came from a northeasterly direction, that of the Primitive Methodists was a calculated mission inspired in the first instance from Hull. The advent of Primitive Methodism in the Kendal district was equally deliberately planned by the Silsden mission. Compared with Wesleyan and Primitive Methodist campaigns those of the post-Revival Congregationalists were sporadic, localised, and fairly frequently short-lived. The Wesleyan Association took its stand by secession from within the county, and apart from an early brief success in Kendal its strength was ever in the Appleby district. So far as we have been able to discover the only secession from Old Dissent to Methodism which resulted in the formation of a Methodist society was that at Ravenstonedale where the Independent minister, William Hassell, became a Wesleyan in 1838 and seceded with a group of his supporters to form the Wesleyan cause in the village. In time the Methodists gained by Inghamite decline, and in some areas Friends joined them on the closure of their meetings. In 1837 some orthodox Kendal Friends, having left their meeting on doctrinal grounds, formed Kendal's Brethren assembly after a brief sojourn in the Scotch Chapel; and in 1843 Guthrie seceded from the latter.

Apart from the efforts of Congregationalists from Lancaster in the Kirkby Lonsdale area, post-Revival missions to Westmorland appear to have come round rather than through comparatively populous Lancashire. It is tempting to speculate upon the possibility that Lancashire's unitarian strength constituted a bulwark against itinerant evangelical trinitarians.[1] Certainly Congregational orthodoxy in Westmorland was saved as much by Scottish theological influences in the person of, and *via* the students of, James Scott, as by anything else. (And this despite the apparent coolness of some ministers towards their brethren from north of the border. Thus, for example, in a letter written from Kendal to Philip Doddridge on 8th November 1740, John Birkett informs Doddridge that the latter's suggestion that Thomas Gillespie should serve at Hartbarrow for six months 'on Mutual Trial' has been accepted, even though 'the Presbyterian Ministers of this North Class of Westmorland and Cumberland are extremely prejudiced against Scotch ministers in general' – a prejudice conceivably occasioned by the Scots' 'unwillingness to embrace every Wanton, Wild, Novel Notion that is broach'd now-a-days'.)[2] On the other hand, however, Lancashire responded generally favourably to Wesley and his assistants. We must therefore simply note the fact that post-Revival forays into Westmorland did not come *via* Lancashire to any large degree.

The Westmorland Lake District was the last area of the county to be successfully missioned by the Methodists and Congregationalists, and during the present century the former have trebled their membership in the Ambleside circuit. We may perhaps attribute this in part to the increasing accessibility of the Lakes, and to their increasing attractiveness to the retired. In contrast, the drift from the land during the same period has resulted in the reduction by one third of Methodist membership in the Kirkby Stephen and Appleby area. The Baptists, ever predominantly rural in Westmorland, have suffered even more: their membership has fallen by one half during the present century.

We must now note three inter-denominational unions which have affected Westmorland nonconformists, and greet one new arrival on the county's nonconformist scene.

The first union affected the members of the Appleby circuit of the United Methodist Free Church who, in 1907 became part of the United Methodist Church, whose other constituents were the Methodist New Connexion and the Bible Christians. A still wider Methodist union was consummated in 1932, when the Wesleyan, Primitive and United Methodists came together. In common with their brethren the land over the Westmorland Methodists set up joint committees to make suitable arrangements for the prosecution of the work of the new Church in their locality. Officers were appointed, preaching plans were devised, and the question of redundant buildings was raised. Our estimate of Methodist membership in Westmorland at the time of Methodist union is as follows: Wesleyan, 1,495; Primitive, 662; United, 97 – a total of 2,254.

The third union was somewhat different in kind. On 8th October 1972 the union of the Presbyterian Church of England and the Congregational Church in England and Wales was ratified. Though not as significant numerically as the earlier Methodist unions, this union is of considerable theological important in that it has required that ability to cross confessional boundaries which has for so long eluded the English – and others. Thus St. John's, Kendal, and the county's erstwhile Congregational churches came together in the United Reformed Church. The congregation of St. John's subsequently united with that of Zion, Kendal, and the St. John's building has been demolished.

Newest on the scene are the Pentecostalists. There are Assemblies of God churches at Kendal and Elterwater. The work in Kendal was begun on 15th September 1942 when a Welsh evangelist, David B. Owen, preached in the Labour Hall. When he left the district about seven months later there were about 22 converts and a congregation of approximately 40. In 1970 membership was about 25 at Kendal and 20 at Elterwater.

In 1970 Westmorland Congregationalists returned a total of 300 members, as follows: Kendal 149, Ravenstonedale 23, Stainton 6, Troutbeck Bridge 10, Carver Memorial, Windermere, 112. In the same year the Kendal Unitarians claimed 56 members, and St. John's Presbyterian Church 232. Christian Brethren membership in the county for 1970 may be estimated thus: Ambleside 16, Bowness 20, Kendal 100, Kirkby Stephen 10 – a total of 146.

More recent Quaker meetings to have come and gone are Arnside (1890–1910) and Gillingate, Kendal (1890–1940). The only newer meeting to survive to this day is that at Kirkby Stephen (1927–). There was, however, a long tradition of Quaker worship in the Kirkby Stephen area prior to 1927, as witness the old meeting which first gathered at the Toll Gate, where a meeting house was erected in 1709, and subsequently met at Narthwaite until its closure in 1907. The 1970 *Book of Meetings* records a total of 216 Friends in Westmorland, as follows: Kendal 146, Kirkby Stephen 14, Preston Patrick 24, Ambleside 32 – a total of 216. The school at Stramongate remained under private Quaker management until 1927, in which year a board of governors was appointed comprising representatives of the Old Boys' Association, the Bryan Lancaster Trustees, the London Yearly

Meeting and the Westmorland Quarterly Meeting, and the residents of Kendal. The depression of the 1930's finally deprived the school of necessary funds and pupils, and it closed in 1932. The premises are still used as a school by the Local Education Authority.[3]

As for the Baptists, in 1915 services were still held at Kelleth, Sunbiggin, Crosby Garrett, Great Asby, Winton and Kirkby Stephen though those at Kelleth and Sunbiggin were to cease before the 1914–18 War ended. The four last named witness to this day, constituting the *one* Westmorland Baptist church.[4] They belong to the Northern Baptist Association, and in 1970 they returned 39 members, 36 children, and 9 young people between the ages of 14 and 20.

Some impressions of the state of Methodism in the county by 1970 may be gained from the following tables:

Location	First chapel erected or purchased	Date of present chapel	Original denomination of present chapel	Membership in 1970
AMBLESIDE AND WINDERMERE CIRCUIT				
Ambleside	1845	1898	Wesleyan	87
Bowness		1883	Wesleyan	65
Windermere		1867	Wesleyan	52
Grasmere		1874	Wesleyan	22
KENDAL CIRCUIT				
Kendal, Stricklandgate	1808	1883	Wesleyan	287
Old Hutton[5]		?	Wesleyan	29
Levens		1891	Wesleyan	21
Arnside		1899	Wesleyan	137
Kirkby Lonsdale		1834	Wesleyan	37
Lupton[5]		?	Wesleyan	9
Holme		1923	Wesleyan	18
Milnthorpe		1904	Wesleyan	47
Storth		1937	Methodist	41
Lower Fellside		1899	Primitive	61
Barbon		1889	Wesleyan	16
Staveley	1836	1876	Wesleyan	35
Beckfoot		1872	Primitive	11
Kendal, Sandylands Road		1954	Methodist	83
Whinfell		1903	Primitive	7
KIRKBY STEPHEN, APPLEBY AND TEBAY CIRCUIT				
Appleby	1823	1904	Wesleyan	128

Location	First chapel erected or purchased	Date of present chapel	Original denomination of present chapel	Membership in 1970
Hilton and Murton		1837	Wesleyan	5
Dufton	1839	1905	Primitive	9
Bolton	1820	1926	United	17
Long Marton		1818	Wesleyan	13
Kirkby Thore	1812	1828	Wesleyan	13
Milburn		1854	Wesleyan	34
Crackenthorpe[5]		?	Primitive	1
Knock		1873	Wesleyan	4
Espland Hill		1866	Wesleyan	15
Ormside[5]		?	?	5
Great Asby		1859	United	7
Catherine Holme		1879	Wesleyan	6
Warcop	1821	1872	Wesleyan	18
Sandford		1848	United	10
Kirkby Stephen, Centenary		1839	Wesleyan	36
Kirkby Stephen, Fletcher Hill	1865	1905	Primitive	46
Soulby	1836/9	1893	Wesleyan	32
Bleatarn		1907	Wesleyan	7
Kaber	1859	1891	Primitive	24
Mouthlock	1831	1910	Primitive	8
Nateby		1873	Wesleyan	19
Mallerstang		1878	Wesleyan	7
North Stainmore		1864	Primitive	13
Winton		1897	Wesleyan	24
Brough, High Street		1905	Wesleyan	39
Brough Sowerby		1897	Primitive	31
Crosby Garrett		1882	Wesleyan	22
Tebay	1865	1885	Primitive	37
Orton		1833	Wesleyan	31
Gaisgill		1841	Wesleyan	16
Newbiggin on Lune	1837 (P.M.)	1939	Methodist	36
Ravenstonedale		1839	Wesleyan	34
Kings Meaburn		1932	Wesleyan	5
Crosby Ravensworth		1875	Wesleyan	32
Greenholme		1898	Primitive	7
Maulds Meaburn		1878	United	9
KIRKOSWALD CIRCUIT				
Temple Sowerby		1872	Wesleyan	27
PENRITH CIRCUIT				
Glenridding	1842	1890	Wesleyan	11

Location	First chapel erected or purchased	Date of present chapel	Original denomination of present chapel	Membership in 1970
Shap	1845	1931	Wesleyan	33
Cliburn		1832	Wesleyan	5
Morland		1819	Wesleyan	0
Newby		1853	Wesleyan	2
Great Strickland		1887	Wesleyan	10
Sleagill		1925	Methodist	18
Tirril		1879	Wesleyan	7
Helton		1867	Wesleyan	16
Bampton Grange		1877	Wesleyan	20
SEDBERGH CIRCUIT				
Fell End		1861	Wesleyan	15
			TOTAL	2029

We may now determine the entire nonconformist membership in Westmorland in 1970, and the percentage of that membership to the county's population:

Friends	216
Congregationalists	300
Baptists	39
Methodists	2029
Unitarians	56
Presbyterians	232
Brethren	146
Pentecostalists	45
	3063

Thus in 1970 4.2% of the population of Westmorland was in membership of nonconformist churches.

The following tables will make further statistical points plain:

	Membership in 1900	Membership in 1970	% change	County pop'n 1900	% of pop'n	County pop'n 1971	% of pop'n
Friends	210	216	+2.86	64303	.337	73836	.296
Congregationalists	500	300	–40.00		.805		.412
Baptists	79	39	–50.60		.126		.054
Methodists	2288	2029	–11.30		3.670		2.790

The population of Westmorland increased by 13.27% between 1900 and 1971. The membership figures of none of the denominations matched this, and the Friends alone showed any increase at all. Our next table will enable us to see whether what happened to the denominations in Westmorland is representative of what happened to the same denominations nationally:[6]

	1900	1970	% change	G.B. & I. 1900	% of pop.	G.B. & I. 1971	% of pop.
Friends	19903	22563	+13.36	38387268	.051	55521534	.041
Cong.	415664	282758	–32.00		1.080		.510
Baptists	353258	274871	–22.20		.920		.496
Methodists	803793	645834	–19.60		2.100		1.162

The population of the land increased by 44.635% between 1900 and 1971. The membership figures of none of the denominations matched this, and once again the Friends alone showed an increase. Their increase in Westmorland was not so great as in the country at large. The Congregationalists and Baptists declined more swiftly, and the Methodists more slowly in Westmorland than in the country at large.

We do not wish to over-emphasise the importance of statistics, partly because we cannot guarantee that ours are flawless – though they are as accurate as we can make them; but mostly because they tell comparatively little of the tale. And even when we have mentioned Francis Howgill the imprisoned; Christopher Jackson the ejected; Elizabeth Gaunt the martyred; John Wesley and Benjamin Ingham, itinerants extraordinary; James Sneath, Stephen Brunskill and Thomas Batty, determined evangelists – and so many more, our record is still incomplete. To approach a comprehensive roll of honour we must refer to that faithful, unknown company of farmers and shepherds, shop keepers, railway workers and lead miners, housewives and children. And of these those who opened their homes for worship, and those who tramped arduous miles in all weathers as lay preachers deserve special praise. To a large extent Westmorland nonconformity is *their* memorial.

NOTES

I : INTRODUCTION

1. Richard S. Ferguson, *Cumberland and Westmorland M.P.'s*, London and Carlisle, 1871, p.10.
2. *N & B* I, p.9
3. Cf. the remarks of Chancellor Ferguson quoted in *ECW* I, p.125.
4. *ECW* I, p.26 5
5. *Ibid.*, p.32.
6. Nightingale quoting *Reliquiae Baxterianae, ibid.*
7. J. H. Colligan, 'Nonconformity in Cumberland and Westmorland', *CHST* III, 1907/8, p.227.
8. D.K.K. [i.e. H. W. Duncan] *Reminiscences of Persons and Places in Kendal Sixty Years Ago*, Kendal, 1890, pp.84–6, 111–2, 139. The old St. George's Chapel stood on the site now occupied by the Public Library. Whitelock served there from 1807–1822. SO *KK*, p.297.

II ORIGINS

1. Henry J. Cadbury, 'The Antiquity of the Quakers', *The Friends' Quarterly*, 1953, p.112.
2. For a marked tendency in this direction see e.g. A. Taylor, *A History of the English General Baptists*, 2 vols. 1818.
3. The tradition is recounted in a ms. letter of Thos. Iveson dated 27/11/1909. This is one of a number of ms. letters and reports loaned by Mr. E. Palmer, Secretary of the Northern Baptist Association. See also Charles W. Kent, 'History of the Westmorland [Baptist] Churches', *The Baptist Outlook*, March 1913, p.50.
4. *ONK*, pp.4–5.
5. *ECW* I, p.84.
6. *Ibid.*, pp.84–5.
7. For Cole see *ECW* II, pp.1014–28.
8. *ECW* I, p.48
9. For this incident and its aftermath see *ONK*. pp.16–22.
10. *ECW* I, pp.82–3. For Oliver Cromwell (1599–1658), see *DNB* V, pp.155–86.
11. These are set out in full in *ECW* I, pp.109–12.
12. For Masy see *ECW* II, pp.877–928.
13. For Higginson see *DNB* IX, p.824: *ECW* II, pp.1075–89.

14. For Nayler (1617?–1660) see *DNB* XIV, pp.130–3; *EQL*, p.68; *EQW*, pp.602–3; *BQ* and *SPQ*, *passim.*
15. *CR* pp.125–6.
16. For Samuel Cole see *ECW* II, pp.972–5.
17. For Wilkinson see *ECW* II, pp.1212–4.
18. See W. T. Whitley, *Baptists of North-West England*, 1913, pp.109 ff.
19. *ECW* I, p.107.
20. J. H. Colligan, 'Nonconformity in Cumberland and Westmorland', *op. cit.*, p.225.
21. *ECW* I, pp.88–107 is vitally important for an understanding of this issue. Nightingale reproduces the Agreement in full.
22. For Richard Gilpin (baptised Kendal 23/10/1625, died 13/2/1690) see *DNB* VII, pp.1260–1; *ECW passim; CR*, pp.223–4.
23. For Fleming (1633–1701) see *DNB* VII, p.275; and *The Memoirs of Sir Daniel Fleming*, transcribed by R. E. Porter and ed. W. G. Collingwood, Cumberland and Westmorland Antiquarian and Archaeological Society Tract Series XI, Kendal 1928.
24. For Taylor (1618–1682) see *DNB* XIX, pp.446–7; *EQL*, P.74; *EQW*, pp.612–3; for Howgill (1618–1699) see *DNB* X, pp.120–1; *EQL*, p.64; *EQW*, pp.597–8; Will Hayes, *Gray Ridge*, Meopham Green 1942; for Audland (1630–63/4) see *EQL*, p.51; *EQW*, pp.581–2; and many references to all of them in *BQ* and *SPQ*.
25. *FPT*, p.244. Cf. W. C. Braithwaite, 'The Westmorland and Swaledale Seekers in 1651', *JFHS* V, 1908, pp.3–10. Braithwaite here draws attention to papers which once belonged to Philip Swale of Hartforth, and which are now at the North Yorkshire County Record Office, Northallerton. They provide evidence of the continuity of personalities and ethos which existed between the Seeker separatist communities and the Society of Friends which absorbed them. The Swale papers are described in 'Records of the Richmond Monthly Meeting of the Religious Society of Friends', North Riding Record Office *Report*, 1966, pp.25–38. See especially pp.30–5 for details of the Swale family and of the links between them and the Whartons. See also, G. F. Nuttall, 'Overcoming the World : the Early Quaker Programme' (Presidential Address), in *Sancity and Secularity : the Church and the World*, Studies in Church History X, ed. Derek Baker, 1973, pp.160–1.
26. See Hugh Barbour, *The Quakers in Puritan England*, New Haven and London, 1964, pp.83–4. Barbour points out that e.g. in Westmorland 12 only out of 41 parishes had schools in 1645.
27. *The Journal of George Fox* [hereinafter, *Journal*] a revised edn. by John L. Nickalls, Cambridge 1952, p.58. For Fox see *DNB* VII, pp. 557–62; *EQL*, p.60; *BQ* and *SPQ passim.*
28. Cadbury quoting Fox's *Epistles* (1698), 'The Antiquity of the Quakers', *op. cit.*, p.116. For Fox's understanding of 'Truth' we may refer to his *Catechisme for Children:* Q: What is Truth? A: Christ, which doth enlighten every man, which cometh into the world and that is the Truth which every man is enlightened withal.

29. The Westmorland Seekers are described by Rufus M. Jones, *Studies in Mystical Religion*, 1909, chap. XIX, especially pp.461–3. Braithwaite draws on this account in *BQ*, pp.25–7.
30. *Journal*, p.104.
31. *FPT*, p.253. Cf. W. C. Braithwaite, 'The Westmorland and Swaledale Seekers in 1651', *op. cit.*, pp.9–10; *BQ*, pp.17–8; *ONK*, p.32. The three ministers with whom Taylor disputed the question of baptism are not named in the foregoing, or in *DNB*, or in Robert Barrow's Testimony to Thomas Taylor in *Truth's Innocency and Simplicity shining through the Conversion. . . of Thomas Taylor*, 1697.
32. R. M. Jones, *op. cit.*, p.463.
33. *FPT*, p.244.
34. *Journal*, p.107.
35. *Ibid.*, p.109.
36. For Quaker remains in the district see Ernest E. Taylor, *Some Quaker Associations*, 1924; Elfrida Vipont Foulds, *The Birthplace of Quakerism*, revised edn. 1968; and the series of articles in *The Friend* as under note 132 below. For a local account of Fox's arrival in the area see the extract from the Sedbergh Monthly Meeting Minutes in *EQW*, pp.60–1
37. *Journal*, p.110.
38. See E. Taylor, *The Valiant Sixty*, 1951, p.26; E. Vipont, *George Fox and the Valiant Sixty*, 1975. For John Camm (1604?–56) see *DNB* III, p.756; *EQL*, p.55; *EQW*, p.587; for Thomas Camm (1641–1707) see *DNB* III, p.756; and references to both in *BQ* and *SPQ*.
39. *Journal*, p.110.
40. For Burrough (1634–63) see *DNB* III, pp.443–4; *EQL*, p.40; *EQW*, p.586; *BQ* and *SPQ passim*; E. Brockbank, *Edward Burrough, a Wrestler for Truth*, 1949.
41. Quoted in *SPQ*, p.444.
42. *Journal*, p.111.
43. *Ibid.*, pp.117–8. William Lampitt was ejected from Ulverston in 1662. Ten years later he became a licensed Independent preacher at his own house. See *CR*, pp.313–4.
44. Thomas Fell (1598–1658), though never fully convinced himself, opened his home, Swarthmore Hall, to the Quakers. Through his wife Margaret (1614–1702), who married Fox in 1669, the Hall became the headquarters of the Quaker evangelistic thrust. For M. Fell see *DNB* VI, pp.1161–2; *EQL*, p.59; *EQW*, pp.592–3; *BQ* and *SPQ passim*; Isabel Ross, *Margaret Fell, Mother of Quakerism*, 1949; Helen G. Crosfield, *Margaret Fox of Swarthmore Hall*, n.d. but preface has 1913.
45. *Journal*, p.123.
46. For Christopher Taylor see *DNB* XIX, p.467; *EQW*, p.612.
47. *Journal*, p.144.
48. For Benson, Puritan colonel, ex-mayor of Kendal, who was convinced at Judge Fell's house, see *EQL*, p.52; *EQW*, p.583.

49. See the duplicated pamphlet by the Revd. G. W. Brassington, *The Grayrigg Quakers* (Studies in the Social History of Grayrigg, no. 3), n.d. Copy in the Public Library, Kendal.
50. *Journal*, p.145.
51. For Whitehead (1636?–1723) see *DNB* XXI, pp.98–101; *EQL*, p.76; *EQW*, p.615; *BQ* and *SPQ*, *passim.*
52. See W. Nicholls, *The History and Traditions of Ravenstonedale, Westmorland*, II (i.e. the second and enlarged edition), Manchester and London, n.d. (but Preface to the first edn. is dated 14/9/1877), pp.71–3.
53. *BQ*, p.111. There are numerous references to Westmorland in *EQL*. Among the most interesting are those relating to Nayler. Thus, for example, in [November 1652] he writes to Margaret Fell from [Appleby] : 'The people are very brutish, kept under a woeful, drunken, sottish priesthood, but some begin to discern them'. (Letter 10). Again, in a letter to George Fox from [Appleby, February 1653] Nayler relates that he 'was made after their sessions to refuse their diet, and since to live upon bread and water . . . Oh dear friends rejoice with me, for I see that to be taken out of all created things is perfect freedom'. (Letter 21). Dr. Nuttall has pieced together Nayler's itinerary from the letters, and shows that Nayler was in Westmorland in 1653 as follows: 5th July, Appleby; 7th July, Stricklandhead; c. 21st July, Kendal; 22nd or 23rd July, Hutton; 24th July, Grayrigg; 27th July, Murthwaite; 28th July, Wath (now in Newbiggin on Lune parish: 'Quaker Garth' extant here); 31st July; Shap; 1st August, Sleagill; thence to Co. Durham; 10th August, Shap; 12th or 13th August, Newby. See *EQL*, 91–2.
54. *Journal*, p.139. Cf. *BQ*, pp.108–9. For the 'priests' ' petition see Besse's *Sufferings* I, p.301.
55. So Cotton Mather, *Magnalia Christi Americana*, 1702, bk. III pt. ii, cap. l, pp.75–6. Cited by G. F. Nuttall, *Sanctity and Secularity*, p.160. Cf. *ECW* II, p.1077. Nightingale points out that Mather is mistaken in using the word 'first' since Higginson refers in his first pamphlet to an anti-Quaker publication entitled, *The Querers and Quakers cause at the Second Hearing.* In *EQW* p.64 *A Brief Relation* is said to be 'at most the third' anti-Quaker tract. Nightingale and Nicolson and Burn refer to Higginson's *two* pamphlets; and it appears that there was a sequel to *A Brief Relation.* The latter confess to knowing of the existence of but one copy of them, and for this reason they provide a full summary of their contents. (*N & B* I, pp.536 ff.) Their account done, the authors comment ruefully on the Judge at Nayler's trial, Anthony Pearson: 'This same Justice Pearson (to show how catching is enthusiasm) afterwards turned Quaker [i.e. in 1653], and writ a book against tithes'. *Op. cit.*, p.539. They further feel that opposition to Quakers has a counter-productive effect, and that 'By letting them alone, they are coming about of themselves; and in the next generation most of

their formal [*sic*] absurdities will be no more heard of'. *Op. cit.*, p.540. For Pearson (1628–1670?) see *DNB* XV, pp.606–7; *EQL*, pp.69–70; *EQW*, p.605. He returned to the Anglican fold after 1660, thereby retaining his status.

56. *ECW* II, p.1077.
57. *Journal*, pp.147–8.
58. *Ibid.*, p.165.
59. *The Quakers Shaken etc.*, 1653. Cf. *BQ*, p.147; *ECW* I, pp.127–8. In the same publication Gilpin criticised Robert Collison, who presumably was among Fox's earliest converts at Kendal, for asserting that Christ displayed lack of trust in God when he prayed, 'Why hast thou forsaken me?' in Gethsemene. To maintain this, argues Gilpin, was to undermine Christ's capacity as redeemer. See *ONK*, pp.34–5; H. Barbour, *The Quakers in Puritan England*, p.118.
60. See *A Further Discovery etc.*, 1654, pp.83–4.
61. Published London, 1654. Copy in the Public Library, Kendal.
62. For Brownsword and his works see *ECW* II, pp.942–54; *ONK* chap. III; *KK*, pp.263–4; L. Hetherington, 'The Quaker–Jesuite', in *The Kendal Mercury and Times*, 22/4/1904 and cf. *Westmorland Quaker Records*, pp.62–6. This is a book of cuttings housed at the Friends' Library, London. It includes, pp.1–61, a series of articles from *The Kendal Mercury and Times*, 17/1/1902 etc. These articles comprise selections from Quaker records housed at Kendal Record Office, together with notes from other sources). Brownsword was succeeded by Richard Tatham, and he by Michael Stanford who, in his epitaph in Kendal Parish Church is described, not without good reason, as *fanaticorum malleus*. See *Westmorland Quaker Records*, pp.17–9. A ms. in the Bodleian Library, which Braithwaite dates c.1677, shows that about 200 out of 800 Friends who were convicted as Popish recusants came from Westmorland. See *JFHS* XI, 1914, p.135 for Braithwaite's suggestion of 1669 as being the date of the document, and *SPQ*, pp. 100-1 for his revised opinion.
63. Quoted in *ONK*, p.27.
64. E. E. Taylor, *The Valiant Sixty*, p.11.
65. *BQ*, p.464. Braithwaite quotes a Quaker tract in Lord Somers's Collection vii 246 (1660): 'there hath suffered imprisonments, putting in the stocks, whippings, loss of goods, and other abuses for keeping a good conscience towards God and man, before the King came into England, 3170 persons'.
66. R. S. Ferguson, *Cumberland and Westmorland M.P.'s*, pp.1–6, and especially pp.6–8 for a description of the scanty manner in which the restored monarch repaid the loyalists.
67. *BQ*, pp.135–7. A letter on the subject of the Fund, written by George Taylor to Margaret Fell on 26th February 1654/5 may be seen in *EQW*, pp.475–6. Taylor and Thomas Willan, both of Kendal, became Treasurers of the Fund. For them see *EQL*, pp.74 and 77 respectively, and *EQW*, pp.612 and 616 respectively.

68. *Westmorland Quaker Records*, p.22.
69. *BQ*, pp.325–6.
70. *Ibid.*, p.328.
71. *Journal*, pp.313–4
72. *Ibid.*, p.374.
73. *Ibid.*, p.453.
74. *Ibid.*, p.455. For Sir Philip Musgrave (1607–1678) see *DNB* XIII, pp.1318–9.
75. H. J. Cadbury, 'George Fox's Later Years', appended to *Journal*, p.730.
76. For Sterne (1596?–1683) see *DNB* XVIII, pp.1108–10; Carleton (1598?–1685) see *DNB* III, pp.1101–2.
77. For Hyde (1609–74) see *DNB* X, pp.370–89.
78. For the ministers here listed see *CR*. For individuals see further as follows: Greenwood: *ECW* II, pp.997–9; *ONK*, pp.83–4; Jackson: *ECW* II, pp.1094–7 and 1284; Josiah Walker Nicholson, *History of Crosby Garrett Westmorland*, Kirkby Stephen 1914, p.61; Bryan Dale, *Yorkshire Puritanism and Early Nonconformity*, 1909, p.86; and sources under 'Ravenstonedale' below; Langhorne: *ECW* II, 1219–20, 1230, 1400; Roberts: *ECW* II, pp.1224–6; Wallace: *ECW* II, pp.976–8; *ONK*, pp.81–3; Camelford: *ECW* II, p.1289; *ONK*, pp.438–9; *LN*, p.291; Dalton: *ECW* II, pp.1190–4; Dodson: *ECW* II, pp.1101–9; Fothergill: *ECW* II, pp.1203–8; *ONK*, p.84, Smith: *ECW* II, pp.1028–31; *ONK*, p.84. Mr. John Creasey of Dr. Williams's Library has kindly supplied me with a copy of the relevant sections of two lists 'which Calamy borrowed from Morrice' (so *CR*, p.xxxv). The lists are identical, and Wallace/Wallis appears as Mallace in both. The lists comprise: John Dalton of Shape, Dodsham of Russendale, Francis Higgison of Kirby Stephen, Christopher Jackson of Crosby on the Hill, Christopher Lanhorn of Ascam, Timothy Roberts of Barton, John Mallace of Evisham, James Greenwood of Hutton near Kendal. For the text of the Act of Uniformity and of the Declaration of Breda see F. G. Healy, *Rooted in Faith*, 1961.
79. *CR*, P.xiii.
80. *CR*, p.xlii. Believing as they did that the church comprises baptised believers, and that ministers ought to be supported not by tithes, but by the voluntary contributions of their people, the Baptists had not for the most part felt able to put themselves in positions from which they *could* be ejected. General Baptist ministers were more consistent in this matter than their Particular brethren. Even so, a small number only of the latter were liable to ejectment. See W. T. Whitley, *A History of the British Baptists*, 1923, p.160; and his 'The Relation of Baptists to the Ejectment', in *The Ejectment of 1662 and the Free Churches*, n.d. but 1912, pp.75–96. Cf. E. A. Payne, 'Baptists and the Great Ejectment', in E. A. Payne and N. S. Moon, *Baptists and 1662*, 1962. Dr. Payne suggests (p.15) that John Skinner (for whom see *CR*, p.444) seems to be an

exception to Whitley's claim that all ejected Baptists were Calvinists. Certainly Skinner attended the General Baptist Assembly of 1689. He is not listed, however, in Adam Taylor's Index of General Baptist Ministers, *op. cit.* I, pp.486–9.

81. For Marsden see *ECW* II, pp.959–60.
82. For the staunch nonconformist, Philip Lord Wharton (1613–96) of Wharton Hall near Ravenstonedale see *DNB* XX, pp.1318–21; *ECW* I, pp.74–5; Bryan Dale, *The Good Lord Wharton*, enlarged edn. 1906; G. F. Trevallyn Jones, *Saw-Pit Wharton*, Sydney, 1967.
83. See *ECW* II, pp.1371–2.
84. *Ibid.*, pp.1358–62.
85. For Kendal see *ONK passim; LN*, pp.278–90; *ECW* II, pp.1287–8; *KK, passim;* D.K.K., *op. cit., passim*; Alexander Gordon, ed., *Freedom after Ejection*, Manchester 1917, p.295; Frank Wilson, 'Rise and Progress of Sunday Schools in Kendal', a paper read before the Sunday School Teachers' Conference, September 1880, and reprinted from *The Kendal Mercury and Times*. Copy in the Public Library, Kendal.
86. For Whitehead (d.1678–9) see *CR* p.526.
87. For Benson (d.1692) see *CR*, p.49.
88. For Frankland (1630–98) see *DNB* VII, pp.626–9; *ONK*, pp.113–95 and (his students) 532–612; *CR*, pp.211–2; T. Whitehead, *History of the Dales Congregational Churches*, Keighley 1930, pp. 46–56; H. McLachlan. *English Education under the Test Acts*, 1931, pp.62–70 and *passim*. K. W. Wadsworth, *Yorkshire United Independent College*, 1954, pp.19–29; J. W. Ashley Smith, *The Birth of Modern Education*, 1954, pp.17–21.
89. For Issot (d. 1687/8) see *ONK* pp.199–200. The following students of Frankland served in Westmorland: Timothy Puncheon and James Mitchell, Ravenstonedale; William Pendlebury, Kendal; John Atkinson, Crook; John Atkinson, Stainton. See *ONK* pp.570, 576–7, 603–4, 605.
90. For Heywood (1630–1702) see *DNB* IX, pp.385–7.
91. For Jollie (1629–1703) see *DNB* X, pp.974–6; *CR*, p.301.
92. For Timothy Jollie (1659?–1714) see *DNB* X, pp.976–7.
93. See *ONK*, p.172.
94. For which see K. W. Wadsworth, *op. cit.*, pp.29–33; J. W. Ashley Smith, *op. cit.*, pp.109–111.
95. For Thomas Lamplaugh (1615–91) see *DNB* XI, pp.472–3. For Thomas Rokeby (1631?–1699) see *DNB* XVII, pp.153–4.
96. Quoted in *ONK*, p.97.
97. See G. Lyon Turner, *Original Records of Early Nonconformity under Persecution and Indulgence* II, p.641; *ECW* II, pp.1371–2.
98. *ONK*, p.234.
99. For Elizabeth Gaunt (d.1685) see *DNB* VII, pp.951–2; T. Crossby, *The History of the English Baptists*, 1738–40, III pp.185–93; Bogue and Bennett, *History of Dissenters* II p.306. Contrary to the Ravenstonedale window, she met her death on 23rd October.

100. Nicholls, *op. cit.*, p.103, quoting Hume's *History of England* VIII, 1793, p.234.
101. For Keach (1640–1794) see *DNB* X, pp.1142–3.
102. See 'Distressed Sion Relieved, 1689', *The Baptist Quarterly* V, 1930–1, p.229.
103. For Ravenstonedale see *LN*, pp.309–18; *ECW* II, pp.1095–6, 1284; A. Gordon, *Freedom after Ejection*, p.338; Nicholls, *op. cit.*, pp.105–122; T. Whitehead, *op. cit.*, pp.89–105; Phyllis L. Woodger and Jessie E. Hunter, *The High Chapel*, Kendal 1962; J. H. Colligan, 'Nonconformity in Cumberland and Westmorland', *op. cit.*, pp.217–9; *LR*, 219–20.
104. For Stainton and Crook see *LN*, pp.291–5; *ECW* II, pp.1289–90; *ONK*, chap. XXXIII.
105. For Hulme see *ONK*, chap. XIX.
106. For Dearnley and Thorneley see *ONK*, chap. XXI. The Presbyterian Fund, established in 1689, was supported by both Presbyterians and Independents until the latter withdrew their support in 1693.
107. The following are among many accounts of the Kaber Rigg Plot: *ECW* I, pp.115–7; *LR*, pp.140–1; *SPQ*, pp.29–31; R. S. Ferguson, *Early Cumberland and Westmorland Friends*, 1871, pp.4–5; and his *Cumberland and Westmorland M.P.'s*, pp.28–32; Martin W. Holdgate, *A History of Appleby*, Appleby 1956, p.43; Nicholls, *op. cit.*, pp.98–102; Nicholson, *op. cit.*, pp.58–60; and especially, Francis Nicholson, 'The Kaber Rigg Plot, 1663', *Transactions of the Cumberland and Westmorland Antiquarian and Archaeological Society*, 1911, pp.212–233. For relevant documents see e.g. *Extracts from State Papers*, Second Series, Friends' Historical Society, 1911, pp.175–6, 177, 185–6. The Fleming *Memoirs* ed. W. G. Collingwood (p.79) are clear that Appleby was the place of Atkinson's execution, on 18th March 1663.
108. E. E. Taylor, 'A Page of Quaker History', *Friends' Quarterly Examiner* CXXV, 1898, pp.29–40. Cf. his *The Valiant Sixty*.
109. *Ibid.*, p.33.
110. *Ibid.*, p.40. It is interesting to note in passing that whereas Taylor maintains that in general 'in outward circumstances Friends of this Quarterly Meeting were comfortably off, or they could not have so long met the heavy distraints made upon their goods . . . (p.30), Barbour, having studied local Quaker wills concludes that 'these men were not well off economically, however sturdy and independent'. (*The Quakers in Puritan England*, p.91) No doubt some were comfortably off, but many made great sacrifices for their faith. What is more interesting is the diversity of *type* found among the early Friends. Scholars such as Thomas Taylor; gentry such as Benson; men like Richard Crewdson, 'a very poor man'; schoolmasters, yeomen, tradesmen, widows – they all found in Quakerism what they had found nowhere else. Quakers have never covered a wider cross-section of the population than they did in their early years.

111. E. E. Taylor, *The Valiant Sixty*, p.36. Cf. *SPQ*, pp.130, 664; *JFHS* XXII, 1925, p.96; *ONK*, p.218. All refer to the Fleming mss., p.201. For an example of Fleming's earlier zeal in hounding nonconformists see his letter to Secretary Joseph Williamson of 19th August 1670, quoted in *LR*, p.29 and in *ONK*, p.97.
112. Copy in the Public Library, Kendal.
113. Written 10th August 1663 and quoted in *LR*, P.27.
114. For which see *SPQ*, chap. XI.
115. *FPT*, p.256. A further cause of friction was Fox's sanctioning of Monthly and Quarterly Meetings for women. He refers to the Westmorland Women's Meeting in a letter written in 1674. See *Journal*, p.692.
116. *Westmorland Quaker Records*, p.26.
117. *JFHS* XLVIII, 1956–8, p.224.
118. *Westmorland Quaker Records*, p.24. Cf. *KK*, p.400.
119. T. R. Newbold, 'Friends' Meeting House, Kendal', *The Friend*, 18/10/1895, p.677.
120. So. E. E. Taylor, *The Valiant Sixty*, p.91.
121. For details see L. John Stroud, *The History of Quaker Education in England, 1647–1903*, a thesis presented in the University of Leeds, 1944.
122. For Lawson (1630–91) see *DNB* XI, pp.738–9; *EQL*, p.66; *EQW*, p.600; *BQ*, *passim*.
123. *JFHS* VI, 1909, p.169. A school at Warcopp *[sic]* is listed in 1670. See *JFHS* VII, 1910, p.19.
124. *JFHS* XXXIII, 1936, pp.55–6.
125. *JFHS* XXX, 1933, p.40.
126. See *The Friend*, 18/8/1893, p.537.
127. This work has sometimes been ascribed to Thomas Lamb, the General Baptist.
128. For the school see pamphlets, prospectuses etc. in the Friends' Library, London, and 'A History of Stramongate School' in *The Old Stramonian* (The Journal of the Old Boys and Old Girls of Stramongate School, Kendal 1698–1932), No. 9, October 1967, pp.84–95. Miss S. J. Macpherson kindly drew my attention to the latter.
129 *BQ*, p.512.
130. *CHST* III, 1907–8, p.301. Cf. G. Lyon Turner, *op. cit.*, II, p.642; *ECW* II, p.1329. No other nonconformist group in Westmorland reported conventicles in 1669. For Gilbert Sheldon (1598–1677) see *DNB* XVIII, pp.24–6.
131. E. E. Taylor, *The Valiant Sixty*, p.116.
132. The following is the list of sources from which we have drawn statistical and other information concerning Quaker dispersal through the county: *LR, passim; Meeting Records* for Westmorland at the Friends' Library, London; *Dissenting Meeting Houses*, 1836, *Dissenters' Places of Worship*, 1853, and *Churches, Chapels, &c*, 1882 – all in the Library of the House of Commons; J. W. Braithwaite, *Guide to Kirkby Stephen, etc.*, Kirkby Stephen,

1884; T. F. Bulmer, ed., *History, Topography, and Directory of Westmorland*, 1885; David M. Butler, 'Meeting Houses Built and Meetings Settled : Answers to the Yearly Meeting Queries, 1688–1791', *JFHS* LI, 1965–7, pp.174–211; Edward H. Milligan, 'Meetings Settled, Discontinued or United'. Summary of Reports to London Yearly Meeting, 1834–1890', *JFHS* XLIX, 1959–61, pp.97–103; J. H. Colligan, 'Nonconformity in Cumberland and Westmorland', *op. cit.*, pp.212–228; *N & B*; and the following articles by Thomas R. Newbold, which appeared in *The Friend* as follows: Tirril, 14/7/1893, pp.457–8; Strickland, 28/7/1893, p.489; Morland, 14/8/1893, pp.505–6; Newby Head Burial Ground, 18/8/1893, pp.537–8; Mislet, Windermere, 25/1/1895, pp.57–8; Preston Patrick, 13/9/1895, p.599; Kendal, 18/10/1895, p.677; Grayrigg, 27/3/1896, p.199. Records of Strickland Monthly Meeting from 1675 onwards are at the County Record Office, Kendal. See also David M. Butler, *Quaker Meeting Houses of the Lake Counties*, 1978.

III THE EIGHTEENTH CENTURY

1. For Pendlebury (?–1729) see *ONK*, pp.238–48.
2. For Chorlton (1666–1705) see *DNB* IV, pp.275–6; J. W. Ashley Smith, *The Birth of Modern Education*, pp.105–6; *ONK*, p.559.
3. For Audland (?–1714) see *ONK*, pp.249–61.
4. For Rotheram (1694–1752) see W. Turner, *Lives of Eminent Unitarians*, I, pp.359–66; *DNB* XVII, p.298; *ONK*, pp.292–318; *LN*, pp.281–2; for his academy and pupils see *ONK*, pp.319–29 and 613–34; H. McLachlan, *English Education Under the Test Acts*, pp.188–91; J. W. Ashley Smith, *op. cit.*, pp.106–7.
5. For Dixon (1680?–1729) see *DNB* V, pp.1031–2; W. Turner, *op. cit.*, I, p.356; J. W. Ashley Smith, *op. cit.*, pp.106–7.
6. For Walker (1734?–1807) see *DNB* XX, pp.515–6; *ONK*, p.632. John Blackburn, who served at Ravenstonedale for a short period from summer 1745, was the only one of Rotheram's students to hold a Westmorland pastorate. See *ONK*, p.615.
7. *ONK*, p.306.
8. For Caleb Rotheram the younger (1732–1796) see *ONK*, pp.334–65.
9. For Joseph Priestley (1733–1804) see *DNB* XVI, pp.357–76.
10. For Christie (1748–1823) see *DNB* IV, pp.287–8.
11. *ONK*, p.350.
12. *Ibid.*, p.360.
13. *Ibid.*, p.361.
14. See J. H. Colligan, 'The Provincial Meeting of Cumberland and Westmorland', *CHST* IV, 1909/10, pp.159–68.
15. For Ainslie (1760–1834) see *DNB* I, p.188; *ONK*, p.515.
16. For Harrison (1761–1833) see *ONK*, pp.366–94.

17. See *ONK* chap. XXIV: 'Was Kendal Chapel "Originally Orthodox?"'
18. For orthodox Presbyterianism in Kendal see John Inglis, *Reminiscences of the United Presbyterian Church of Kendal for One Hundred Years*, Kendal 1865; Marshall N. G. Gray, *Presbyterianism in Kendal: a Historical Sketch*, Kendal, 1908.
19. For Burder (1752–1832) see *DNB* III, pp.294–5; H. Foster Burder [his eldest son], *Memoir of the Rev. George Burder*, 1833; *LN*, *passim*.
20. H. F. Burder, *op. cit.*, p.69; *LN*, p.227.
21. H. F. Burder, *op. cit.*, p.116.
22. Daniel Gibbons studied at the Countess of Huntingdon's College, Trevecca, and in October 1777 Burder could write that Gibbons hab been preaching in Lancaster for some months (H. F. Burder, *op. cit.*, p.45). By the end of 1779 he was at Ulverston, where he was ordained on 5th July, 1780. He also preached at Bootle, Cumberland, 1779–80. He died on 11th December 1785, aged 30. See *The Life and Times of Selina Countess of Huntingdon*, by a member of the houses of Shirley and Hastings, (hereinafter: *Life and Times*) 2 vols. 1840, II, p.465; *LN*, pp.194, 227, 257, 258, 285, (Nightingale appears to exaggerate when, on p.285, he states that Gibbons was 'for many years' minister at Ulverston); *EM* N.S.X., 1832, p.555; *The Congregational Magazine*, 1822, p.164.
23. H. F. Burder, *op. cit.*, p.81; *LN*, p.285. This theatre stood at the NE corner of Market Place, and was subsequently employed as the Working Men's Library. As we shall see, a congregation of the Countess of Huntingdon's Connexion and the Wesleyans also rented it in their turn. The theatre should not be confused with that in Woolpack Yard which the orthodox Presbyterians took in 1823. For Kendal's theatres see D.K.K., *op. cit.*, pp.112–5.
24. H. F. Burder, *op. cit.*, p.103; *LN*, p.286.
25. James Kenworthy (?– 16th June 1828) studied at Heckmondwike academy. He was minister at Warrington before 1794, and remained there until 1797. After a pastorate at New Chapel Horwich (1797–1825) he retired, and died aged 80. See *LN* I, p.286; III, p.107, IV, p.229; V, p.166; VI, pp.144–7, 267; *EM* II, 1794, p.252.
26. *ONK*, p.284. In a footnote Nicholson and Axon refer to two further protrinitarian pamphlets by Atkinson.
27 *LN*, p.295. For Scott (1710–83) see K. W. Wadsworth, *Yorkshire United Independent College*, pp.11, 18, 40–55; T. Whitehead, *History of the Dales Congregational Churches*, pp.56–7, 123–5; J. W. Ashley Smith, *op. cit.*, p.187.
28. H. F. Burder, *op. cit.*, p.83. Cf. *LN*, p.295; J. H. Colligan, 'The Provincial Meeting of Cumberland and Westmorland', *op. cit.*, p.165.
29. See G. F. Nuttall, 'The influence of Arminianism in England', in his *The Puritan Spirit*, 1967, pp.67–80.
30. *ONK*, p.289, citing *CHST* III, p.95.
31. In *JFHS* I, 1903/4, pp.121–3. For further remarks upon the changing spirit see *SPQ*, pp.xxxii–iii.

32. *ONK*, p.275. Apparently, the Oxford Methodists, with their high view of the sacraments etc., were not utterly persuaded of the right of Quakers to the name 'Christian'. Thus Ingham could inquire of Wesley on 30th November 1734 'whether it be convenient or lawful for a Christian to dwell with a Quaker when under no necessity'. See L. Tyerman, *The Oxford Methodists*, 1873, p.60. For Ingham see below n.38.
33. *ONK*, p.441.
34. See Thomas Taylor, *An Historical Sketch of the Baptist Church at Tottlebank*, (1864), reprinted 1946.
35. W. T. Whitley, *A Baptist Bibliography* I, 1916, p.152. Cf. *ONK*, p.289.
36. *ONK*, pp.615–6, 628, 633–4.
37. See 'Daniel Noble', *The Baptist Quarterly* I, 1922/3, pp.135–8.
38. For Ingham (1712–1772) see *DNB* X, p.434; *Life and Times* I, pp.242–75; L. Tyerman, *op. cit.*, pp.57–154; David F. Clarke, 'Another "Son to Susanna", Benjamin Ingham, 1712–72', *PWHS* xxxviii, 1973, pp.170–6. For Inghamites in Westmorland R. W. Thompson, *Benjamin Ingham and the Inghamites*, Kendal, 1958, is valuable. See also 'Benjamin Ingham in Westmorland' in the 1952 brochure of the Annual Convention of the Fellowship of Inghamite Churches; copy in the Public Library, Kendal. There are Inghamite membership rolls, letters, sundry documents and hymn books at the County Record Office, Kendal. The early baptismal and burial registers are there on microfilm, the originals being at the Public Record Office, London. Wesleyan-Inghamite relations are helpfully summarised by A. W. Harrison, *The Evangelical Revival and Christian Reunion*, 1942.
39. For Potter (1674?–1747) see *DNB* XVI, pp.216–7.
40. A. W. Harrison, *op. cit.*, p.105.
41. L. Tyerman, *op. cit.*, p.106. For John Wesley (1703–1791) see *DNB* XX, pp.1214–25; for Charles Wesley (1707–1788) see *DNB* XX, pp.1209–13.
42. So Tyerman, *op. cit.*, p.122 and *DNB*. But Thompson, *op. cit.*, p.28 has May.
43. Lady Margaret, of whom it was said that 'the greatest glory that shone in her was that of religion, in which she was not only sincere, but excelled', (*Life and Times* I, p.250 – wrongly numbered 259 *ad. loc.*) was born in 1700 and died on 30th April 1768. For the Countess of Huntingdon (i.e. Selina Hastings) (1707–01) see *DNB* IX, pp.133–5, and *Life and Times.*
44. For Glas (1695–1773) see *DNB* VII, pp.1296–7; for Sandeman (1718–1771) see *DNB* XVII, pp.744–5. Also L. Tyerman, *op. cit.*, pp.140–5.
45. In 1752 James Allen of Gayle near Hawes, then aged 18, became an Inghamite preacher. See Tyerman, *op. cit.*, pp.136–7, citing *EM*, XXII, 1814, pp.306–7. William Batty and his younger brothers Lawrence and Christopher were all Inghamite preachers. Their home

was at Newby Cote near Settle. See Tyerman, *op. cit.*, p.123. Cf. *Life and Times* I, pp.246–7, where we are informed that William Batty was ordained pastor (in succession to Ingham) at Wheatley in 1760, and that 'He died suddenly, without a sigh or a groan, December 12, 1787, aged 72'. In a letter of 13th November 1778, G. Burder states that he had heard Batty preach on Romans 1:18, and that 'His sermon was very sound, and he discovered a surprising knowledge of Scripture'. H. F. Burder, *op. cit.*, p.71.

46. *Life and Times* I, pp.269–70.
47. R. W. Thompson, *op. cit.*, pp.52–3.
48. *Ibid.*, p.77.
49. *Life and Times* I, p.270. Cf. R. W. Thompson, *op. cit.*, p.36.
50. R. W. Thompson, *op. cit.*, p.79.
51. So R. W. Thompson, *op. cit.*, p.46. This appears to refer to a period post 1829 (from which date Independents occupied the chapel). A John Capper, who also kept a school, was Independent minister at Kirkby Stephen, 1824–35. We know that he supplied the cause at Brough in 1826, and he is said to have supplied Birks in 1829 (*LN*, p.321). Capper began his career as an agent for Lancashire Congregational Union. See R. Slate, *A Brief History of the Rise and Progress of the Lancashire Congregational Union, etc.* 1840, pp.27–8; *LN*, pp.95–6, 306, 321; *LN* IV, pp.37–8; W. G. Robinson, *A History of the Lancashire Congregational Union, 1806–1956*, Manchester, 1955, pp.35–6. In *The London Christian Instructor or Congregational Magazine* VII, 1824, p.716, he appears as M. Capper, Thompson says that he met his death by drowning. He has no obituary in *CYB*.
52. Quoted in the *Nicholson ms.* and the Inghamite brochure. Cf. R. W. Thompson, *op. cit.*, p.89.
53. See G. H. Bancroft Judge, 'The Beginnings of Methodism in Ambleside', *PWHS* XXV, 1945/6, pp.107–22. Cf. Myles Holmes, *History of Methodism in Ambleside*, Farnworth, 1873. Copy in the Public Library, Kendal. It is instructive to compare Wesley's lack of success in Ambleside with his conspicuous success in Wednesbury, another much visited town. He was in Wednesbury on some 33 occasions and, rioters notwithstanding, had gathered a society of over 100 within a week of his first visit. A preaching house was opened as early as 1760, and Wednesbury became the mother of Black Country Methodism. See J. F. Ede, *History of Wednesbury*, Wednesbury, 1962, pp.211–2.
54. *VCH*, Cumberland, II, 1905, p.107.
55. For Whitefield (1714–1770) see *DNB* XXI, pp.85–92. The four quotations here used are from the following letters reproduced in Whitefield's *Works*, 1771/2, II: DCCCXLII, p.356; DCCCXLIII, p.357; DCCCXLIV, p.358; DCCCXLVI, p.360. Curwen (*KK*, p.354) states that in 1745 Whitefield began a sermon in Kendal Market Place as follows: 'Oyez, Oyez, Oyez ye loyal men of Kendal, having heard with what readiness you have enlisted under the banners of

His Majesty, King George, to defend him and his throne against all Enemies, I am proud to come among you, since I also hold a commission, not from any earthly potentate, but from the King of Kings, with power to enlist you under the banner of the cross, and lead you to triumph over the world, the flesh, and the devil'. But Whitefield was in America throughout 1745.

56. *Life and Times* I, p.157.
57. *KK,* p.354. Whitefield expressed *his* opinion in a letter written to Lady Huntingdon from Kendal on 10th August 1751: 'Thanks be to GOD, the seed sown in Kendal last year hath sprung up, and borne fruit'. *Works* II, p.421, Letter DCCCCIV.
58. Taken from the *Nicholson ms.* For Osbaldeston (1690–1764) see *DNB* XIV, pp.1169–70. He was said to be 'rich, indolent, and chiefly non-resident', and when he was translated to London it was, says Hurd, 'to nobody's joy that I know of'. His successor at Carlisle, Charles Lyttelton, found the diocese in a very low state.
59. T. A. Bainbridge; 'John Wesley's travels in Westmorland and Lancashire North-of-the-Sands', *Transactions of the Cumberland and Westmorland Antiquarian and Archaeological Society,* LII, 1953, pp.106–13.
60. Bainbridge quotes from F. W. MacDonald's edition of *The Journal of the Rev. John Wesley,* 1906, and the bracketed numerals in his text and ours refer to this.
61. G. H. Bancroft Judge, *op. cit.*, p.109.
62. A copy of his autobiography, *The Life of Stephen Brunskill of Orton,* 1837, may be seen at the Public Library, Kendal. The Introduction, in which Brunskill declares his sense of obligation to 'retrace the kind providence that has attended me through every period of my life' is dated 1st July, 1812. For a brief account of Brunskill see Bulmer, *History, Topography, and Directory of Westmorland,* 1885, pp.252–3.
63. *Ibid.*, p.5.
64. *Ibid.*
65. *Ibid.*, p.6.
66. *Ibid.*
67. *Ibid.*
68. *Ibid.*, p.7.
69. *Ibid.*, p.11.
70. *Ibid.*, p.13.
71. *Ibid.*, p.17.
72. *Ibid.*, p.19.
73. *Ibid.*, p.30.
74. *Ibid.*, p.33ff.
75. *KK,* p.355.
76. Brunskill's *Life,* p.60.
77. *Ibid.*, p.61.
78. *Ibid.*, p.68.
79. *Ibid.*, pp.69–70.

80. The account of the last four years of Brunskill's life is by another writer.
81. *LN*, pp.286–7. The list of Trevecca students, including Mr. Gray, appears in *Life and Times* II, pp.112–3. Gray (? – 3rd September 1808) supplied Bootle in 1782; served at Kendal from 1782–95; and at Bootle, 1795 until his death at the age of 53.
82. *LN*, p.287.
83. *Life and Times* II, p.466.
84. *Ibid.*, p.443.
85. *Ibid.*, p.467.
86. *Ibid.*, p.466.
87. *Ibid.*, p.467.
88. Lady Huntingdon's *MSS* at Cheshunt College, Cambridge, F1/579. I am grateful to the late President of Cheshunt College, the Revd. J. E. Newport, for permission to quote from three of the letters in this collection.
89. *Ibid.*, F1/594.
90. *Ibid.*, F1/720.
91. Brunskill's *Life*, p.35.
92. *Ibid.*, p.39.
93. *Ibid.*, p.40.
94. D.K.K. *op. cit.*, pp.84–5. J. F. Curwen states (*KK*, p.34) that Robinson (d.1845), a hosier and grocer in Kirkland, rented a room in South Road as an Independent Methodist chapel, and that afterwards the room was used by the Mormons. Since D.K.K. appears more knowledgeable as to the theology of Robinson's group, and since the (Arminian) Independent Methodists, though they first formed a union in 1805, did not finally adopt their present name until 1898, we may conclude that Curwen's capital 'I' is misleading, and that he does not have the Independent Methodist denomination in mind. See J. Vickers, *History of Independent Methodism*, Newton-le-Willows, 1920.
95. Quoted by Henry J. Cadbury, *John Woolman in England*, 1971, pp.86–7. Cadbury notes that George and Jane Crosfield, members of the Preston Patrick meeting, lived at Low Park near End Moor, Preston Richard, and that the house is extant. He further observes: 'Woolman had met Jane Crosfield during her travels in America. On 12 mo. 1760 he wrote to her in the evening after some Friends meetings that they had both attended at Rancocas and Mount Holly, New Jersey, meetings which she also mentions in her itinerary under the same date'. *Op. cit.*, p.100, citing mss. in the possession of George B. Crosfield. Cf. *JFHS* III, 1906, p.31.
96. H. J. Cadbury, *op. cit.*, p.99, citing A. M. Gummere (ed.) *The Journal and Essays of John Woolman*, New York, 1922, p.141.
97. *Ibid.*, p.110.
98. *Ibid.*, p.102. The letter written from Lancaster on 22nd October 1772.
99. *Ibid.*, p.135.

100. For John Dalton (1766–1844) see *DNB* V, pp.428–34; *LPQ* II, pp.762–8; also J. T. Marsh, *Old Quaker Dalton*, reprinted from Vol. III of *Memoirs & Proceedings of the Manchester Literary and Philosophical Society*, Session 1968/9, Manchester, n.d.
101. *DNB* V, p.429.
102. *N & B*, p.80.
103. P. Sangster, *Pity My Simplicity*, 1963, p.110. This is an engaging study of 'The Evangelical Revival and the Religious Education of Children 1738–1800'. For local Sunday Schools see Frank Wilson, *Rise and Progress of Sunday Schools in Kendal*, a paper read before the Sunday School Teachers' Conference, September 1880. Reprinted from the *Kendal Mercury and Times*. Copy in the Public Library, Kendal. Cf. *ONK, passim.*
104. *ONK*, p.352, citing *State of Sunday Schools in Kendal*, 1787.
105. For Robinson see *ONK*, pp.373–4.
106. F. Wilson, *op. cit.*, p.5.

IV: THE NINETEENTH CENTURY

1. Pamphlets concerning the renovation and re-opening are at the Public Library, Kendal.
2. Kindly loaned by the Revd. J. P. Monkhouse. Mr. Monkhouse placed some most useful documents and notes at our disposal. Methodist plans, minute books, etc. may be seen at the County Record Office, Kendal. Supplementary materials are at the John Rylands University Library of Manchester. The Revd. G. W. Dolbey kindly supplied statistical information concerning the Methodists, and the Methodist ministers named in our preface filled several other gaps in the story. For Methodist indentures for the north of the county see *LR passim.* For details of circuits see T. Galland Hartley, ed., *Hall's Circuits and Ministers*, 1925. For Hutton Roof see P. Gaskins, *Methodism in Hutton Roof*, n.d., c.1975.
3. See the Fell End centenary pamphlet by J. P. Monkhouse.
4. *Wesleyan Methodist Magazine*, 1867, p.276. Report by the Revd. Walter Briscombe. A footnote to the report speaks of the great service rendered by Lake District Methodism by the late superintendent minister, the Revd. S. Atkinson. For Grasmere Methodism see the centenary brochure, *Grasmere Methodist Church, 1874–1974.*
5. *Ibid.*, 1870, p.468. Report by the Revd. James Morrison.
6. *Ibid.*, 1872, p.1045. Report by the Revd. John Burdon.
7. *Ibid.*, 1873, p.662. Report by the Revd. T. J. Macartney.
8. Copy at John Rylands Library, Manchester.
9. *Wesleyan Methodist Magazine*, 1864, p.468.
10. E.g. that at Long Marton, which celebrated its centenary in 1918. The Revd. Samuel Chadwick, President of the Conference, gave the address. See the report in the *Penrith Observer*, 29/10/1918. For

Casson, to whom reference is made in this paragraph see A. Steele, *The Life and Labours of Hodgson Casson*, 1853.

11. Baptist materials are comparatively slight. In addition to the few published sources mentioned below, and to minutes at Baptist Church House, we have drawn upon ms. letters and reports kindly made available by Mr. E. Palmer, Secretary of the Northern Baptist Association; the *Nicholson ms.*; the local knowledge of Miss W. M. Burra; and upon two short articles: 'The Baptists in North Westmorland', *Cumberland and Westmorland Herald*, 10/2/1917, and 'Baptist History of the North' by W.M.B., *The Northerner*, January 1964. As long ago as the early years of the century writers were lamenting the loss of early Brough records.
12. For Whitfield see *EM* XVI, 1808, p.493.
13. For Kay (21/6/1777 – 22/9/1847) see *EM* IX, 1801, p.374; X, 1802, p.425n; *LN*, pp.283, 288; *LN* IV, p.11.
14. For the Unitarian Baptismal Register see *ONK*, pp.489–94.
15. Quoted by R. W. Thompson, *op. cit.*, p.1. For William Romaine (1714–95) see *DNB*, XVII, pp.175–7. For Burder's reaction to Inghamite decline see H. F. Burder, *op. cit.*, pp.60–1, 70–1.
16 Abel Stevens gives the figure of 84 in his *History of the Religious Movement of the Eighteenth Century called Methodism*, 1878, I, p.307. Tyerman concurs (*op. cit.*, p.145), and on p.154, quoting from the *Wesleyan Times* of 14/12/1863, he provides locations and statistics as follows: Wheatley 56; Winewall 41; Kendal 27; Nottingham 25; Salterforth 21; Bulwell 17; Tadcaster 14; Howden 11; Wibsey 10; Leeds 9; Rothwell 8; Haslingden 8; Todmorden 5. The book, *Historical Sketches of the Inghamite and Old Scots Independent Churches*, 1813, quoted by R. W. Thompson (*op. cit.*, p.94) agrees with Tyerman, but adds meetings at Thinoaks and Birks, though recording a membership figure for neither. It also supplies the names of the elders as follows: Wheatley: John Walker, farmer, and John Winterbottom, weaver; Winewall: Henry Bannister, weaver; Kendal: John Huck, farmer; Nottingham: John Green, and Isaac Bagley, fell monger; Salterforth: Henry Holgate, weaver; Bulwell: Robert Horrocks, Isaac Pattern, drawer; Tadcaster: Benjamin Wood, and George Holling, tailor; Howden: John Biggs; Wibsey: James Garrs, weaver; Leeds: Joseph Nicholson, book-keeper. *Life and Times* I, p.275 has, 'out of upwards of *eighty* flourishing churches only thirteen remained!'. This writer, Tyerman and Stevens almost certainly blur the distinction between 'chapel' and 'meeting'.
17. See Tyerman, *op. cit.*, p.154; Thompson, *op. cit.*, pp.80, 86. For the Scottish situation see J. T. Hornsby, 'John Glas: His Later Life and Work', *Records of the Scottish Church Society*, VII, 1940; and H. Escott, *A History of Scottish Congregationalism*, Glasgow, 1960, pp.17–36. The Old Scots Independents had 12 churches in Scotland and 1 in London, comprising 501 members. The Inghamites brought 252 members into the wider fellowship.
18. *KK*, p.102.

19. L. Tyerman, *op. cit.*, p.154.
20. *LN* is indispensable for 19th century Congregationalism. See also for Kirkby Stephen: *LR*, p.151; Bulmer, *op. cit.*, p.194; Braithwaite, *op. cit.*, p.170; Whitehead, *op. cit.*, pp.268–79; Temple Sowerby: *LR*, p.165; Brough: *LR*, p.108; Little Asby; Whitehead, *op. cit.*, pp.281–7; Kirkby Lonsdale: Whitehead, *op. cit.*, pp.322–9. In his *The Story of the Lancashire Congregational Union 1806–1906*, Manchester, n.d., but preface has 1906, Nightingale presents a table (p.193) of 'Churches in other unions, etc., which have been, or still are, aided [i.e. by the Lancashire Union]', from which we extract the following:

Name of Church	Number of years	Total amount £ s. d.	Notes
Milnthorpe and Burton	1818–1845: 26 years	1065 0 0	Church dissolved; building being private property, sold in 1866
Wray, Bentham, Ingleton, etc.	1818–1819: 2 years	59 4 0	Abandoned
Little Asby	1892–1906: 15 years	400 0 0	Still aided
Kirkby Lonsdale	1815–1906: 83 years	3052 0 0	Still aided
Kendal	1861–1866, 1892–1906: 21 years	754 0 0	Still aided

Boque and Bennett give 2 Presbyterian, 4 Independent, and 3 Baptist congregations in Westmorland in the early 19th century. See *History of Dissenters* IV, p.328.

21. *EM* V, 1797, p.384.
22. Such writers as Colligan find nothing untoward in this mode of government because they argue, more forcibly than we think proper, that the cause was Presbyterian.
23. For Nicholls (1835–1921) see *CYB*, 1922, p.109.
24. *EM* XIX, 1811, pp.323–4.
25. *EM* XX, 1812, p.283.
26. *EM* XXI, 1813, p.227.
27. *EM* XXII, 1814, p.364.
28. *EM* XXIII, 1815, p.464.
29. Temple Sowerby was a home missionary station.
30. *LN*, p.321. The stations in question are not named in the list for 1829 which we shall shortly quote.
31. For Capper see chap. III n.51 above.
32. *EM* NS XLII, 1864, p.478.
33. Cf. R. Slate, *A Brief History of the Rise and Progress of the Lancashire Congregational Union*, 1840, pp.37–8. For France see *LN*, p.231; *EM* NS XXXII, 1854, pp.652ff; and his somewhat confused

obituary in *CYB*, 1855, pp.214–6. For his subsequent career see E. E. Cleal, *The Story of Congregationalism in Surrey*, 1908, p.259.

34. For John Cockin (1783–1861) see *CYB* 1862, pp.226–7. His father, Joseph Cockin (b. 1755), a student at Heckmondwike under James Scott, ministered with great acceptance at Thornton and Square, Halifax. On 18th August 1811 he addressed a meeting at Heckmondwike, announced the need for home evangelism, and the West Riding Itinerant Society was born. In 1819 the West Riding Home Missionary Society was formed at Wakefield, and in 1854 both societies were absorbed by the Yorkshire Congregational Union. See K. W. Wadsworth, *op. cit.*, p.54; and his *The Yorkshire Congregational Union and Home Missionary Society 1872–1972*, Bradford, 1972, p.9. Also Whitehead, *op. cit.*, pp.35 and 42–4.
35. For Maclean (d. 1840) see *LN*, p.288; *LN* IV, p.153; *The Congregational Magazine*, 1835, p.837; F. J. Powicke, *A History of the Cheshire County Union of Congregational Churches*, Manchester, 1907, p.160.
36. *EM* XXIV, 1816, p.526.
37. For Sharp (1832–1893) see *CYB* 1895, p.229.
38. *EM* XXVIII, 1820, p.236. Cf. *The London Christian Instructor* III, 1820, p.736.
39. *The London Christian Instructor* VII, 1824, p.716.
40. *EM* NS XXI, 1843, p.86. B. Nightingale provides a quotation concerning Milnthorpe in 1824 which illustrates the point that causes with chequered careers were not without their hours of glory: 'Two of the most notorious sinners in the county, who never attended a place of worship for the last thirty years, are not only regular attendants on the Sabbath days, but that in their families, instead of cursing and swearing and lying, they are reading and singing and praying'. *The Story of the Lancashire Congregational Union*, p.166.
41. *Op. cit.*, p.61.
42. *The London Christian Instructor* VII, 1824, p.717.
43. Nightingale quoting Whellan's *History and Topography of Cumberland and Westmorland*, *LN*, p.321.
44. *The Congregational Magazine* NS V, 1829, p.733. It is interesting to observe in passing that this list also includes 'Schools, numbers now educated – *National*, 581, *British*, 40. *Sabbath*, 1500'. Two years previously the same journal's list (p.710) gave: *National*, 199. *British*, 0. *Sunday*, 500'.
45. R. Slate, *A Brief History of the Rise and Progress of the Lancashire Congregational Union; and of the Blackburn Independent Academy*, 1840, p.103. The latter part of Slate's comment holds of the Lake District at the time he writes, but he seems to have overlooked the activities of the Baptists and of the three varieties of Methodists, all of whom were active in other parts of the county in 1840. Unless, of course, he intends us to gather that Congregationalists alone are competent to teach 'the only way of salvation'!
46. John Addison Coombs (d. 1/10/1856, aged 68) has no *CYB* obituary.

Ordained on 26th January 1820, he ministered at Chapel Street, Salford (1818–38) and Ambleside (1839–47).

47. *EM* NS XIX, 1841, p.612–3; Joshua Wilson, *Memoir of the Life and Character of Thomas Wilson,* 1846, p.463. The land cost £140, and in addition Wilson made two £50 donations to the chapel.
48. For Bourne (1772–1852) see *DNB* II, pp.937–8; J. T. Wilkinson, *Hugh Bourne,* 1952. For Clowes (1780–1851) see *DNB* IV, p.591; J. T. Wilkinson, *William Clowes,* 1951. For Primitive Methodism in the county see John Petty, *The History of the Primitive Methodist Connexion,* 1864; H. B. Kendall, *The Origin and History of the Primitive Methodist Church* II, n.d. but c. 1900; W. M. Patterson, *Northern Primitive Methodism,* 1909; 'North Westmorland Primitive Methodism', an article written to celebrate the centenary of the movement in Brough, *Cumberland and Westmorland Herald,* 21/10/1923. Also Primitive Methodist *Minutes,* and sources under n.2 above.
49. See articles entitled, 'Early Quakerism and Early Primitive Methodism', by F. Baker, *The London Quarterly,* 1948, pp.313–23, and *ibid.,* 1949, pp.239–48; J. C. Bowmer, *ibid.,* 1950, pp.148–53, 222–7; G. F. Nuttall, *The Friends' Quarterly* VII, 1953, pp.179–87, reprinted in his *The Puritan Spirit,* 1967, pp.204–13.
50. In his 'History of the Westmorland [Baptist] Churches', *op. cit.,* p.52, Kent notes that Jersey took over from James Sneath on the latter's departure from the Brough *Baptist* circuit in 1848. At some time after an unhappy experience at Nottingham, to which place the Primitive Methodists sent him in 1834, Jersey joined the Baptists. Eventually he emigrated to America.
51. J. T. Wilkinson, *William Clowes,* p.55.
52. *KK,* pp.346–7, 415.
53. F. Wilson, *op. cit.,* p.8.
54. Quoted by Petty, *op. cit.,* p.208.
55 *LR,* p.108, and *passim* for further records relating to Primitive Methodism in the north of the county.
56. J. T. Wilkinson, *Hugh Bourne,* p.139.
57. See Bulmer, *op. cit.,* pp.17–8, and *passim* for other Primitive Methodist causes.
58. *Primitive Methodist Magazine,* 1865, pp.689–91.
59. *Ibid.,* p.689.
60. *Ibid.,* p.690.
61. *Ibid.,* 1867, p.559. Report signed by J.F.B.
62. *The Aldersgate Magazine,* 1903, p.500.
63. See John McKerrow, *History of the Secession Church,* Edinburgh, 1839.
64. For Marshall (1800–28) and other ministers of this church see M. N. G. Gray, *op. cit.,* pp.19ff.
65. The attempts began in Wolverhampton in 1817. Some chapels were attacked, the Independents being prominent in arousing anti-Unitarian feeling.
66. D.K.K., *op. cit.,* p.98. Cf. *ONK,* pp.395–6 and 407–8.
67. D.K.K. delights to tell of the special funeral arrangements that had

to be made for him: an extra-large coffin, and an upstair window removed to allow the passage of the coffin down a ramp into the yard below.

68. For Hawkes (1803–66) see *ONK*, pp.402–27.
69. *ONK*, pp.405–7.
70. Alexander Gordon, *Heads of English Unitarian History*, 1895, p.52.
71. Sources as under n.11 above.
72. These details are reaffirmed in the *Centenary Souvenir Brochure* of Egglesburn Baptist Chapel, 1972 – a pamphlet which reminds us that the Baptist cause spread from Middleton not only into Westmorland, but in other directions as well.
73. We have used the ms. book for 1832 ff. of *Minutes of the Proceedings of the Baptist Home Missionary Society Instituted in London 1797.*
74. D. Douglas, *op. cit.*, p.280. Cf. *LR*, p.109 for the approach of the Brough Baptists to those at Middleton.
75. So Kent, *op. cit.*, p.280. For a report of the formation of the church see *The Baptist Magazine* XXVI (vol. IX, Third Series) 1834, pp. 303–4.
76. *Minutes*, p.72.
77. For Baptist Wriothesley Noel (1798–1873) see *DNB* XIV, pp.534–5; *The Baptist Handbook*, 1874, pp.285–9; D. W. Bebbington, 'The Life of Baptist Noel', *The Baptist Quarterly* XXIV, 1972, pp.389–411.
78. *LR*, p.114.
79. For Crosby Garrett Baptists see Kent, *op. cit.*, part II, pp.88–9; *LR*, p.114; J. W. Nicholson, 'Sketch of Crosby Garrett Church', *The Baptist Outlook*, December 1912, pp.282–4, and his *History of Crosby Garrett Westmorland*, pp.82–7. For the Great Asby indenture see *LR*, pp.92–3. And sources under n.11 above.
80. Bulmer, *op. cit.*, p.365.
81. For the history of the secession and of subsequent developments see H. Smith *et al.*, *The Story of the United Methodist Church*, n.d. but preface has 1932; O. A. Beckerlegge, *The United Methodist Free Churches*, 1957. Conference *Minutes* of the Wesleyan Association and of its successors have been consulted, as have sources under n.2 above. For the leaders of the Methodist groups to be mentioned see *DNB* as follows: Alexander Kilham (1762–98), XI, pp.102–3; William O'Bryan (1778–1868), XIV, pp.784–5; James Everett (1784–1872), VI, pp.951–2; Samuel Dunn (1798–1882), VI, pp.212–3.
82. Beckerlegge, *op. cit.*, p.20, quoting the Association's *Minutes*, 1836, p.18. He adds that the resolution was disregarded by 1842 and rescinded in 1849.
83. J. Walker Nicholson was given access to a memoir of John Dent by Dent's sons, William and J. C. Dent. He used it in compiling his ms., and we know of no other record of the origins of the Wesleyan Association in Westmorland.
84. For reference to Wesleyan Association chapels see *LR passim*;

Bulmer, *op. cit.*, pp.111, 117, 136, 279 and 354. Bulmer erroneously states that the Free Methodist chapel at Bolton originally belonged to the Primitive Methodists. In fact it was Wesleyan.

85. This book, together with other books and plans relating to the Wesleyan Association and its successors in Westmorland, is at the County Record Office, Kendal.
86. See O. A. Beckerlegge, ed., *United Methodist Ministers and their Circuits*, 1968.
87. *Wesleyan Association Magazine*, 1840, p.194.
88. 1852 *Minutes*, p.31.
89. For Isaac Crewdson (1740–1844) see *DNB* V, pp.83–4; *LPQ* I, pp.490–2, 505–8. The issues are discussed by Owen Chadwick, *The Victorian Church* I, 1966, pp.430–2; and especially by Elizabeth Isichei, *Victorian Quakers*, 1970, pp.8–9, 45–53. On p.7 Mrs. Isichei writes, 'there was a clear tendency among evangelicals to neglect the theory of the Light Within – the core of early Quakerism'. With the first part of this statement we may agree, but the latter part is open to misinterpretation, especially by those more familiar with subsequent Quaker mysticism. We should ever remember that for the early Quakers the Light was scripturally interpreted, and that they would not have understood a disjunction between Light and Christ. For the American Hicksites see Robert W. Doherty, *The Hicksite Separation*, New Brunswick, 1967. It is interesting to note that whereas the Beaconites seceded because they deemed their fellow members to be insufficiently evangelical, John Gough (1757–1825) had earlier left the Kendal Society on his embracing unitarianism. In 1815 he was appointed a trustee of Market Place chapel. Despite the fact that an attack of smallpox left him blind before his third birthday, Gough became a notable scholar. He attended the Quaker school in Stramongate, and subsequently became a teacher himself. John Dalton was his most famous pupil, and Wordsworth and Coleridge were among his friends. See H. McLachlan, *Essays and Addresses*, Manchester, 1950, p.62; *ONK*, pp.374, 375, 523–4; *DNB* VIII, pp.277–8.
90. *The Inquirer* I, February 1838, p.64.
91. See *The Proceedings of the Yearly Meeting of the Society of Friends, held in London, from May 22 to June 3, 1837: reprinted with additions, corrections, and explanatory notes, from the 'Patriot' newspaper, etc.*, pp.31–42. At the time Yearly Meeting deliberations were kept secret. The foregoing is a Beaconite revision of the *Patriot's* unofficial report.
92. See F. Roy Coad, *A History of the Brethren Movement*, Exeter, 1968, p.77. Coad points out that the Crewdsons had close family connections with B. W. Newton; and that through local Anglican friends they had contact with Darby's relatives, the Pennefathers of Dublin. For J. N. Darby (1800–82) see *DNB* V, pp.493–4.
93. *Ibid.*, p.215.
94. Bulmer, *op. cit.*, p.18.

95. D.K.K., *op. cit.*, pp.114–5.
96. *Ibid.*, p.134.
97. F. Wilson, *op. cit.*, p.9. Cf. *KK*, p.401.
98. For the details of Guthrie's career see Fergus Ferguson, *A History of the Evangelical Union*, Glasgow, 1876, chaps. XIII and XIV.
99. Quoted by F. Ferguson, *op. cit.*, p.226.
100. *Ibid.*, p.230.
101. *Ibid.*, p.239.
102. The relevant pamphlets are: (i) *New Views – True Views* (not traced by us, but see F. Ferguson, *op. cit.*, p.240); *The 'New Views' – How Met; or the review continued of Doctrinal Questions and Cases under discussion in the Synod of the United Secession Church*, Edinburgh and Kendal, 1843; (iii) *'New Views' as old as the Word of God; Being a Reply to a pamphlet by J. E. Howard, Esq. entitled ' "New Views" compared with the Word of God', and addressed to the believers in Kendal*, London, Glasgow and Kendal, 1843. (ii) and (iii) are at the Public Library, Kendal.
103. Ferguson prints Guthrie's own account of the Synod proceedings and their aftermath, *op. cit.*, pp.243–55.
104. See H. Escott, *op. cit.*, chap. XI, and Ferguson, *op. cit.*, *passim*.
105. So the Lancashire presbytery minutes – see Ferguson, *op. cit.*, p.253. *KK* (p.323) concurs, whilst Gray, *op. cit.*, p.24 records a remnant of 32. Guthrie himself thought that the presbytery figure left 'the impression of a much larger minority than there really was'. Quoted by Ferguson, *op. cit.*, pp.253–4.
106 Zion's records are now at the County Record, Office Kendal. I am grateful to the Revd, Andrew Hodgson for information concerning Zion, and for copies of the Statement and of the letter from which I quote.
107. Quoted by Ferguson, *op. cit.*, p.255.
108. *Ibid.*, p.223.
109. For Groat (1868–1943) see *CYB* 1944, p.427.
110. See William MacKelvie, *Annals and Statistics of the United Presbyterian Church*, 1873, pp.482–3.

V: RETROSPECT, COMPARISONS AND CONTRASTS

1. Thus the 1830 report of the College Committee of Blackburn academy could refer to the fact that in Lancashire 'no fewer than 32 chapels, originally belonging to orthodox Dissenters of the Independent and Presbyterian denominations, have, with their endowments, fallen into the hands of Unitarians'. R. Slate, *op. cit.*, p.130.
2. Doddridge MSS at Dr. William's Library, London, L1/4/101. L1/4/102–4 are also by John Birkett to Doddridge; L1/4/105 is from A. B[irkett] to Doddridge, and L1/4/106, dated 6th April 1759, is from John Birkett to Doddridge's widow, Mercy. For the first five

letters see Geoffrey F. Nuttall, *Calendar of the Correspondence of Philip Doddridge, DD (1702–1751),* HMSO 1979, nos. 652, 1030, 1092, 1135, 1558. For Doddridge (1702–51) see *DNB* V, pp.1063–9. For Gillespie (1708–74), subsequently founder of the Relief Church, see *DNB* VII, pp.1244–5.

3. *The Friend* for 27/12/1929, 3/1/1930 and 17/1/1930 carries letters of Charles J. R. Tipper appealing for £6,000 to save the school, and then announcing that the figure has been 'substantially exceeded'. But not even this success could stave off the impact of the depression.
4. For the bicentenary of Crosby Garrett see *The Cumberland and Westmorland Herald*, 2/10/1954; for the centenary of Great Asby see *ibid.*, 17/11/1962; for the centenary of Winton see *ibid.*, 16 and 23/11/1963.
5. This society does not appear in the 1972 *Statistical Returns* of the Methodist Church Department for Chapel Affairs, though it is on the circuit plan for April–July 1970.
6. In collecting denominational statistics we have aimed at territorial comparability. Thus e.g. the Congregational membership figures include those of the Congregational Union of Church in England and Wales, the Congregational Unions of Scotland and Ireland and the Union of Welsh Independents. The Methodist figure includes that of the Irish Methodist Conference, and the Quaker figure that of the Irish Yearly Meeting. It has proved easier to scale up in this way than to provide figures for England only. The main disadvantage of our method is that a small number of members of each denomination who live in Eire is included in the denominational figures. These are, however, statistically insignificant, and do not seriously disturb our account of the general trends.

LIST OF SOURCES

1 – MISCELLANEOUS SOURCES

Answers to queries given by persons named in the Preface.

Doddridge Mss at Dr. Williams's Library, London.

Lady Huntingdon's Mss at Westminster College, Cambridge.

Ms. chapel minutes of a number of individual parishes.

Ms. letters and notes, Methodist circuit plans, broadsheets, etc. as specified under the following footnotes: Chap. II, notes 3, 128; Chap. III, note 38; Chap. IV, notes 2, 11, 73, 85, 106.

The *Nicholson Ms.*, see p.ix.

2 – PRINTED MINUTES, YEAR BOOKS, etc.

Assemblies in Britain and other parts, 1970.

Assemblies of God Year Book, 1972/3, Nottingham.

The Baptist Handbook, 1871, 1875–6, 1884–

CYB, 1846–1972.

Directory, 1972/3, of the General Assembly of Unitarian and Free Christian Churches.

London Yearly *Epistles,* 1682– , of the Religious Society of Friends.

Minutes of the [Wesleyan] Methodist Conference, 1744–1933.

of the Annual Conference of the Primitive Methodist Connexion, 1820–1915;

then P.M. Year Book including Minutes, 1916–32;

of the Annual Assembly of the Wesleyan Association, 1837–56;

then of the United Methodist Free Churches Annual Conference, 1857–1906;

then of the United Methodist Church Conference, 1907–32.

The Official Handbook of the Presbyterian Church of England, 1971/2.

Religious Society of Friends' *Book of Meetings,* 1970.

3 – REFERENCES, NEWS ITEMS, etc., culled from the following:

The Arminian Magazine, 1778–1797; *then The Methodist Magazine,* 1798–1821; *then The Wesleyan Methodist Magazine,* 1822–1913.

BHST.

The Baptist Magazine, 1810–1904.

The Baptist Outlook.

CHST.

The Cumberland and Westmorland Herald, 1860–
EM
The Friend, 1843–
The Friends' Quarterly Examiner, 1867–1946; *then The Friends' Quarterly*, 1867–1946; *then The Friends' Quarterly*, 1947–
The Inquirer, 1838–40.
JFHS
The Kendal Mercury and Times, 1880–1913. (*Kendal Mercury and Northern Advertiser*, 1841–80.)
The London Christian Instructor or Congregational Magazine, 1818–24; *then The Congregational Magazine*, 1825–45.
The London Quarterly Review, 1853–1931; *then The London Quarterly and Holborn Review*, 1932–68.
The Methodist Magazine, 1819; *then The Primitive Methodist Magazine*, 1821–98; *then The Aldersgate Magazine*, 1899–1932.
The Northerner.
Penrith Observer, 1860–1969.
PWHS.
Transactions of the Cumberland and Westmorland Antiquarian and Archaeological Society, 1866–
The Wesleyan Association Magazine, 1838–57; *then The United Methodist Free Churches Magazine*, 1858–91; *then The Methodist Monthly*, 1892–1907; *then The United Methodist Magazine*, 1908–33.
The Wesleyan Times, 1849–67.
The Westmorland Gazette, 1818–

4 – BOOKS PAMPHLETS and ARTICLES published before 1920 and referred to in the text and/or notes.

A Brief Account of many of the Prosecutions of the People call'd Quakers in the Exchequer, Ecclesiastical, and other Courts, etc., 1736.
A Further Discovery etc., 1654.
Absolute Predestination not Scriptural, c.1708.
Atkinson, John, of Crook and Cockermouth, *A discourse of election etc.*, 1708.
Atkinson, John, of Stainton, *Jesus Christ the Son, essentially the same with God the Father*, 1722.
Axon, Ernest, see Nicholson, F.
Barrow, Robert, Testimony to Thomas Taylor in *Truth's Innocency and Simplicity shining through the Conversion . . . of Thomas Taylor*, 1697.
Besse, Joseph, *Sufferings*, see p.ix.
Bogue, David and Bennett, James, *History of Dissenters*, 4 vols., 1808–12.
Book of Common Prayer, 1662.
Braithwaite, J. W., *Guide to Kirkby Stephen etc.*, Kirkby Stephen, 1884.

Brownsword, William, *The Quaker-Jesuite etc.*, 1660.
Brunskill, Stephen, *Dialogue between a Minister and one of his parishioners and others*, c.1780.
The Life of Stephen Brunskill of Orton, 1837.
Bulmer, T. F., ed., *History, Topography, and Directory of Westmorland*, 1885.
Burder, H. Foster, *Memoir of the Rev. George Burder*, 1833.
Burn, R., see Nicolson, J.
Camm, Thomas, *The Memory of the Rightous Revived*, 1689.
Churches, Chapels, &c., 1882.
Cleal, Edward E., *The Story of Congregationalism in Surrey*, 1908.
Cole, William, *The Perfect Pharisee etc.*, 1654.
Colligan, J. Hay, 'Nonconformity in Cumberland and Westmorland', *CHST*, III, 1907/8, pp.212–27.
'The Provincial Meeting of Cumberland and Westmorland', *CHST*, IV, 1909/10, pp.159–68.
Crewdson, Isaac, *A Beacon to the Society of Friends*, 1835.
Crosby, T., *The History of the English Baptists*, 4 vols., 1738–40.
Crosfield, Helen G., *Margaret Fox of Swarthmore Hall*, n.d. but preface has 1913.
Dale, Bryan, *The Good Lord Wharton*, enlarged edn., 1906.
Yorkshire Puritanism and Early Nonconformity, ed. T. G. Crippen, 1909.
Daye, James, *The Christian's service compleated with honour*, 1752.
Dissenters' Places of Worship, 1853.
Dissenting Meeting Houses, 1836.
'Distressed Sion Relieved, 1689', *The Baptist Quarterly*, V, 1930/31, pp.227–31.
Doctrinal Errors Condemned by the United Associate Synod of 1842, Edinburgh, 1842.
Dodson, Joseph, *Moderation and Charity*, 1719.
D.K.K. [i.e. Mr. H. W. Duncan], *Reminiscences of Persons and Places in Kendal Sixty Years Ago*, Kendal, 1890.
Evans, John, *List of Dissenting Congregations and Ministers in England and Wales*, 1715–29.
Extracts from State Papers, Second Series, Friends' Historical Society, 1911.
Ferguson, Fergus, *A History of the Evangelical Union*, Glasgow, 1876.
Ferguson, Richard S., *Cumberland and Westmorland M.P.'s*, London and Carlisle, 1871.
Early Cumberland and Westmorland Friends, 1871.
Foster, Joseph, *Alumni Oxonienses*, 4 vols. 1887/8; 4 further vols. 1891/2.
Fox, George, *Journal*, see Nickalls, John L.
Catechisme for Children, 1667.
et al., *Saul's Errand to Damascus etc.*, 1653.
Gilpin, John, *The Quakers Shaken etc.*, 1653.
Glas, John, *The Testimony of the King of Martyrs concerning his Kingdom, etc.*, 1727.

Gordon, Alexander, ed., *Freedom after Ejection*, Manchester, 1917.
Heads of English Unitarian History, 1895.

Gray, Marshall N. G., *Presbyterianism in Kendal: a Historical Sketch*, Kendal, 1908.

Guthrie, John, *'New Views' as old as the Word of God, etc.*, London, Glasgow and Kendal, 1843.
'New Views' – True Views, c.1843.
The 'New Views' – How Met, Edinburgh and Kendal, 1843.

Hetherington, L., 'The Quaker-Jesuite', *The Kendal Mercury and Times*, 22/4/1904.

Higginson, Francis, *A Brief Relation of the Irreligion of the Northern Quakers*, 1653.

Historical Sketches of the Inghamite and Old Scots Independent Churches, 1813.

Holmes, Myles, *History of Methodism in Ambleside*, Farnworth, 1873.

Howgill, Francis, *A Lamentation for the Scattered Tribes*, 1656.
with J. Naylor, *A woe against the magistrates, priests, and people of Kendal etc.*, 1654.

Hume, D., *History of England*, VIII, 1793.

Inglis, John, *Reminiscences of the United Presbyterian Church of Kendal for One Hundred Years*, Kendal, 1865.

Jones, Rufus M., *Studies in Mystical Religion*, 1909.

Kendall, H. B., *The Origin and History of the Primitive Methodist Church*, c.1900.

Kent, Charles W., 'History of the Westmorland [Baptist] Churches', *The Baptist Outlook*, March 1913, pp.50–3; *ibid.*, April 1913, pp.87–91.

Lawson, Thomas, *An Appeal to the Parliament concerning the Poor, etc.*, 1660.

MacDonald, F. W., ed., *The Journal of the Rev. John Wesley*, 1906.

MacKelvie, William, *Annals and Statistics of the United Presbyterian Church*, Edinburgh, 1873.

McKerrow, John, *History of the Secession Church*, Edinburgh, 1839.

Mather, Cotton, *Magnalia Christi Americana*, 1702.

Naylor, James, *An Answer to the Booke called The Perfect Pharisee, etc.*, 1654.
with F. Howgill, *A woe against the magistrates, etc.*, 1654.

Newbold, Thomas R., series of articles in *The Friend*, 1893–6. See chap. II, note 132.

Nicholls, W., *The History and Traditions of Ravenstonedale, Westmorland*, II, Manchester and London, n.d. but preface to first ed. is dated 14/9/1877.

Nicholson, Francis, 'The Kaber Rigg Plot, 1663', *Transactions of the Cumberland and Westmorland Antiquarian and Archaeological Society*, 1911, pp.212–33.
with Ernest Axon, *The Older Nonconformity in Kendal*, Kendal, 1915.

Nicholson, Josiah Walker, *History of Crosby Garrett, Westmorland*, Kirkby Stephen, 1914.

'Sketch of Crosby Garrett [Baptist] Church', *The Baptist Outlook*, December 1912, pp.282–4.

Nicolson, Joseph and Burn, Richard, *The History and Antiquities of the Counties of Cumberland and Westmorland*, 1777.

Nightingale, Benjamin, *Lancashire Nonconformity*, 3 vols., Manchester and London, prefaces dated 1890–3.

The Ejected of 1662 in Cumberland and Westmorland, 2 vols., Manchester, 1911.

The Story of the Lancashire Congregational Union 1806–1906, Manchester and London, n.d. but preface has 1906.

Palmer, Samuel, *The Nonconformist's Memorial*, 1803.

Pastoral Address to the Wesleyan Methodist Societies in the Appleby Circuit, by the Ministers, 1855.

Patterson, W. M., *Northern Primitive Methodism*, 1909.

Pendlebury, William, *The practical influences of the speculative doctrine of Christianity demonstrated*, 1706.

Penney, Norman, ed., *The first Publishers of Truth*, 1907.

Petty, John, *The History of the Primitive Methodist Connexion*, 1864.

Principles of Methodism.

Proceedings of the Yearly Meeting of the Society of Friends . . . 1837: reprinted with additions, etc., 1837.

Reliquiae Baxterianae, 1696.

Rotherham, Caleb, *Dissertatio . . . de Religionis Christianae Evidentia, &c.*, 1743.

Sandeman, Robert, *Letters on Theron and Aspasio*, 1757.

Sedgfield, John, *Jehovah Tsidkenu: etc.*, 1726.

Shipley, C. E., *The Baptists of Yorkshire*, 1912.

Shirley and Hastings, Member of the houses of [i.e. A. C. H. Seymour], *The Life and Times of Selina, Countess of Huntingdon*, 2 vols., 1840.

Slate, R., *A Brief History of the Rise and Progress of the Lancashire Congregational Union etc.*, 1840.

State of Sunday Schools in Kendal, 1787.

Steele, A., *Christianity in Earnest as Exemplified in the Life and Labours of Hodgson Casson*, 1853.

Stevens, Abel, *History of the Religious Movement of the Eighteenth Century called Methodism*, 3 vols., 1878.

Taylor, Adam, *The History of the English General Baptists*, 2 vols., 1818.

Taylor, Christopher, *A Warning to the Nation*, 1655.

The Whirlwind of the Lord, 1655.

Taylor, Ernest E., 'A Page of Quaker History', *Friends' Quarterly Examiner*, CXXV, 1898, pp.29–40.

Taylor, Thomas, *An Historical Sketch of the Baptist Church at Tottlebank*, 1864; reprinted Kendal, 1946.

'The Baptists in North Westmorland', *Cumberland and Westmorland Herald*, 10/2/1917.

The Querers and Quakers cause at the Second Hearing, 1653 or earlier.

Turner, G. Lyon, *Original Records of Early Nonconformity under Persecution and Indulgence*, 3 vols., 1911–4.

Turner, W., *Lives of Eminent Unitarians,* 1840, vol. I.

Tyerman, Luke, *The Oxford Methodists,* 1873.

Vickers, James, *History of Independent Methodism,* Newton-le-Willows, 1920.

Westminster Assembly Documents (all of which are reprinted in *The Subordinate Standards and other Authoritative Documents of the Free Church of Scotland,* Edinburgh, 1933.).

The Confession of Faith, completed 1646.

The Larger Catechism, 1648.

The Shorter Catechism, 1648.

The Directory for the Publick Worship of God, 1645.

The Form of Presbyterial Church Government, 1645.

Westmorland Quaker Records, a book of cuttings kept at Friends' Library, London.

Whitefield, George, *The Works of the Reverend George Whitefield,* 6 vols., 1771–2.

Whitehead, George, *Christian Progress of George Whitehead,* 1725.

Whellan, William, *History and Topography of Cumberland and Westmorand,* Pontefract, 1860.

Whitley, W. T., *A Baptist Bibliography,* 2 vols., 1916 and 1922.

Baptists of North-West England, 1913.

'The Relation of Baptists to the Ejectment', in *The Ejectment of 1662 and the Free Churches,* n.d., but 1912, pp.75–96.

Wilson, Frank, *Rise and Progress of Sunday Schools in Kendal,* 1880.

Wilson, Joshua, *Memoir of the Life and Character of Thomas Wilson,* 1846.

5 – BOOKS, PAMPHLETS and ARTICLES published since 1920 and referred to in the text and/or notes.

'A History of Stramongate School', *The Old Stramonian,* No. 9, October 1967, pp.84–95.

Bainbridge, T. A., 'John Wesley's travels in Westmorland and Lancashire North-of-the-Sands', *Transactions of the Cumberland and Westmorland Antiquarian and Archaeological Society,* LII, 1953, pp.106–13.

Baker, F., 'Early Quakerism and Early Primitive Methodism', *The London Quarterly,* 1948, pp.313–23, and *ibid.,* 1949, pp.239–48.

Barbour, Hugh, *The Quakers in Puritan England,* New Haven and London, 1964.

with Arthur Roberts, *Early Quaker Writings,* Grand Rapids, 1973.

Bebbington, D. W., 'The Life of Baptist Noel', *The Baptist Quarterly,* XXIV, 1972, pp.389–411.

Beckerlegge, Oliver A., *The United Methodist Free Churches,* 1957.

Ed., *United Methodist Ministers and their Circuits,* 1968.

'Benjamin Ingham in Westmorland', in the 1952 brochure of the Annual Convention of the Fellowship of Inghamite Churches.

Bowmer, John C., 'Early Quakerism and Early Primitive Methodism', *The London Quarterly,* 1950, pp.148–53 and 222–7.

Braithwaite, William C., *The Beginnings of Quakerism*, 2nd edn. revised by Henry J. Cadbury, Cambridge, 1970.

The Second Period of Quakerism, 2nd edn., prepared by Henry J. Cadbury, Cambridge, 1961.

'The Westmorland and Swaledale Seekers in 1651', *JFHS*, V, 1908, pp.3–10.

Brassington, G. W., *The Grayrigg Quakers*, n.d., duplicated.

Brockbank, E., *Edward Burrough: A Wrestler for Truth, 1634–1662*, 1949.

W.M.B. [i.e. Burra, W. M.], 'Baptist History in the North', *The Northerner*, Jan. 1964.

Burgess, John, *A History of Cumbrian Methodism*, Kendal, 1980.

Methodism in Westmorland, Wesley Historical Society (Cumbrian Branch), 1980.

Cumbrian Methodists, Wesley Historical Society (Cumbrian Branch) and Cumbrian Religious History Society, 1981.

'The Baptists and the Cumbrian religious censuses', *The Baptist Quarterly*, XXIX, 1981, pp.169–77.

Bulter, David M., 'Meeting Houses built and Meetings Settled: Answers to the Yearly Meeting Quaries, 1688–1791', *JFHS*, LI, 1965–7, pp.174–211.

Quaker Meeting Houses of the Lake Counties, 1978.

Cadbury, Henry J., 'George Fox's Later Years', appended to Fox's *Journal*, ed. Nickalls, q.v.

John Woolman in England, 1971.

'The Antiquity of the Quakers', *The Friends' Quarterly*, 1953, pp.112–7.

Centenary Souvenir Brochure of Egglesburn Baptist Chapel, 1972.

Chadwick, Owen, *The Victorian Church*, I, 1966.

Clarke, David F., 'Another "Son to Susanna": Benjamin Ingham, 1712–72', *PWHS*, XXXVIII, 1972, pp.170–6.

Coad, F. Roy, *A History of the Brethren Movement*, Exeter, 1968.

Collingwood, W. G., ed., *The Memoirs of Sir David Fleming*, transcribed by R. E. Porter, Cumberland and Westmorland Antiquarian and Archeological Society Tract Series XI, Kendal, 1928.

Curwen, John F., *The Later Records relating to North Westmorland or the Barony of Appleby*, Cumberland and Westmorland Antiquarian and Archaeological Society Record Series, VIII, Kendal, 1932.

'Daniel Noble', *The Baptist Quarterly*, I, 1922/3, pp.135–8.

Doherty, Robert W., *The Hicksite Separation*, New Brunswick, 1967.

Ede, J. F., *History of Wednesbury*, Wednesbury, 1962.

Escott, Harry, *A History of Scottish Congregationalism*, Glasgow, 1960.

Foulds, Elfrida Vipont, *The Birthplace of Quakerism*, revised edn. 1968.

Gaskins, P., *Methodism in Hutton Roof*, n.d., c.1975.

Grasmere Methodist Church, 1874–1974, Centenary brochure.

Gummere, A. M., ed., *The Journal and Essays of John Woolman*, New York, 1922.

Harrison, A. W., *The Evangelical Revival and Christian Reunion*, 1942.

Hartley, T. Galland, *Hall's Circuits and Ministers,* 1925.
Hayes, Will, *Gray Ridge,* Meopham Green, 1942.
Healey, F. G., *Rooted in Faith,* 1961.
Holdgate, Martin W., *A History of Appleby,* Appleby, 1956.
Hornsby, J. T., 'John Glas: His Later Life and Work', *Records of the Scottish Church Society,* VII, 1940.
Hunter, Jessie E., see Woodger, P. L.
Isichei, Elizabeth, *Victorian Quakers,* 1970.
Jones, G. F. T., *Saw-Pit Wharton,* Sydney, 1967.
Jones, Rufus M., *The Later Periods of Quakerism,* 2 vols., 1921.
Judge, G. H. Bancroft, 'The Beginnings of Methodism in Ambleside', *PWHS,* XXV, 1945/6, pp.107–22.
McLachlan, H., *English Education under the Test Acts,* Manchester, 1931.
Essays and Addresses, Manchester, 1950.
Marsh, J. T., *Old Quaker Dalton,* reprinted from Vol. III of *Memoirs & Proceedings of the Manchester Literary and Philosophical Society,* Session 1968/9, Manchester, n.d.
Matthews, A. G., *Calamy Revised,* Oxford, 1934.
Milligan, Edward H., ' "Meetings Settled, Discontinued or United", Summary of Reports to London Yearly Meeting, 1834–1890', *JFHS,* XLIX, 1959/61, pp.97–103.
Monkhouse, John P., *Centenary Celebrations,* Fell End Methodist Chapel, 1961.
Moon, Norman S., see Payne, E. A.
Nickalls, John L., ed., *The Journal of George Fox,* Cambridge, 1952.
'North Westmorland Primitive Methodism', *Cumberland and Westmorland Herald,* 21/10/1923.
Nuttall, G. F., *Calendar of the Correspondence of Philip Doddridge, DD (1702–1751),* HMSO, 1979.
Early Quaker Letters from the Swarthmore Mss to 1660, unpublished typescript, 1952. Copies at the Friends' Library, Woodbrooke, Birmingham, *et al.*
'Early Quakerism and Early Primitive Methodism', *The Friends' Quarterly,* VII, 1953, pp.179–87, reprinted in his *The Puritan Spirit,* 1967.
'Overcoming the World: the Early Quaker Programme' (Presidential Address), in *Sanctity and Secularity: the Church and the World,* Studies in Church History, X, ed. Derek Baker, 1973.
'The Influence of Arminianism in England', in his *The Puritan Spirit,* 1967.
Payne, Ernest A., 'Baptists and the Great Ejectment', in E. A. Payne and N. S. Moon, *Baptists and 1662,* 1962.
Powicke, F. J., *A History of the Cheshire County Union of Congregational Churches,* Manchester, 1907.
'Records of the Richmond Monthly Meeting of the Religious Society of Friends', North Riding Record Office *Report,* 1966, pp.25–38.

Robinson, W. Gordon, *A History of the Lancashire Congregational Union 1806–1956*, Manchester, 1955.
Roberts, Arthur, see Barbour, Hugh.
Ross, Isabel, *Margaret Fell: Mother of Quakerism*, 1949.
Sangster, Paul, *Pity My Simplicity*, 1963.
Shaw, Thomas, *The Bible Christians 1815–1907*, 1965.
Smith, H. et al., *The Story of the United Methodist Church*, n.d. but preface has 1932.
Smith, J. W. Ashley, *The Birth of Modern Education*, 1954.
Statistical Returns, Methodist Church Department for Chapel Affairs, 1972.
Stroud, L. John, *The History of Quaker Education in England, 1647–1903*, a thesis presented in the University of Leeds, 1944.
The Subordinate Standards and other Authoritative Documents of the Free Church of Scotland, Edinburgh, 1933.
Taylor, Ernest E., *Some Quaker Associations*, 1924.
The Valiant Sixty, 1951.
Thompson, R. W., *Benjamin Ingham and the Inghamites*, Kendal, 1958.
Vipont, E., *George Fox and the Valiant Sixty*, 1975.
Wadsworth, Kenneth W., *The Yorkshire Congregational Union and Home Missionary Society 1872–1972*, Bradford, 1972.
Yorkshire United Independent College, 1954.
Whitehead, T., *History of the Dales Congregational Churches*, Keighley, 1930.
Whitley, W. T., *A History of the British Baptists*, 1923.
and see under 4 above.
Wilkinson, John T., *Hugh Bourne*, 1952.
William Clowes, 1951.
Woodger, Phyllis L. and Hunter, Jessie E., *The High Chapel*, Kendal, 1962.

INDEX OF NAMES

INDEX OF PLACES

INDEX OF PRINCIPAL SUBJECTS